STUFISH

ENTERTAINMENT ARCHITECTURE

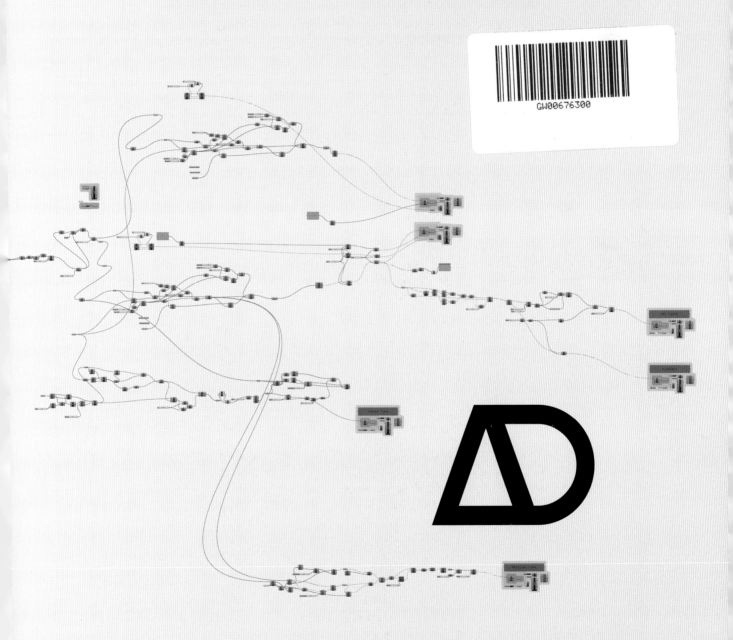

Guest-edited by
RAY WINKLER with NEIL SPILLER

ISSN 0003-8504
ISBN 978 1119 812241

Edited by **Ray Winkler with Neil Spiller**

'The suspension of disbelief and the imagined presence of the other-worldly, in the service of delight or transcendence, is crucial to entertainment architecture.'
— Ray Winkler

Editorial Offices
John Wiley & Sons
9600 Garsington Road
Oxford
OX4 2DQ

T +44 (0)18 6577 6868

Editor
Neil Spiller

Managing Editor
Caroline Ellerby
Caroline Ellerby Publishing

Freelance Contributing Editor
Abigail Grater

Publisher
Todd Green

Art Direction + Design
CHK Design:
Christian Küsters
Barbara Nassisi

Production Editor
Elizabeth Gongde

Prepress
Artmedia, London

Printed in the United Kingdom
by Hobbs the Printers Ltd

Front cover
STUFISH Entertainment
Architects, Dai Show Theatre,
Xishuangbanna, China, 2015.
© STUFISH Entertainment
Architects, photo Raphael
Oliver

Inside front cover
STUFISH, Beyoncé and Jay-Z
'On the Run II' tour, 2018.
© STUFISH

Page 1
STUFISH, National Television
Awards, O2 Arena, London,
2020. © STUFISH

	ARCHITECTURAL DESIGN		
	November/December	Issue	Profile No.
	2021	06	274

Disclaimer
The Publisher and Editors cannot be held responsible
for errors or any consequences arising from the use
of information contained in this journal; the views and
opinions expressed do not necessarily reflect those of
the Publisher and Editors, neither does the publication
of advertisements constitute any endorsement by
the Publisher and Editors of the products advertised.

Journal Customer Services
For ordering information,
claims and any enquiry
concerning your journal
subscription please go to
www.wileycustomerhelp
.com/ask or contact your
nearest office.

Americas
E: cs-journals@wiley.com
T: +1 877 762 2974

**Europe, Middle East
and Africa**
E: cs-journals@wiley.com
T: +44 (0)1865 778 315

Asia Pacific
E: cs-journals@wiley.com
T: +65 6511 8000

Japan (for Japanese-
speaking support)
E: cs-japan@wiley.com
T: +65 6511 8010

Visit our Online Customer
Help available in 7 languages
at www.wileycustomerhelp
.com/ask

Print ISSN: 0003-8504
Online ISSN: 1554-2769

Prices are for six issues
and include postage
and handling charges.
Individual-rate subscriptions
must be paid by personal
cheque or credit card.
Individual-rate subscriptions
may not be resold or
used as library copies.

All prices are subject to
change without notice.

Identification Statement
Periodicals Postage paid
at Rahway, NJ 07065.
Air freight and mailing in
the USA by Mercury Media
Processing, 1850 Elizabeth
Avenue, Suite C, Rahway,
NJ 07065, USA.

USA Postmaster
Please send address changes
to *Architectural Design*,
John Wiley & Sons Inc.,
c/o The Sheridan Press,
PO Box 465, Hanover,
PA 17331, USA

Subscribe to Δ
Δ is published bimonthly
and is available to purchase
on both a subscription basis
and as individual volumes
at the following prices.

Prices
Individual copies:
£29.99 / US$45.00
Individual issues on
Δ App for iPad:
£9.99 / US$13.99
Mailing fees for print
may apply

Annual Subscription Rates
Student: £93 / US$147
print only

Personal: £146 / US$229
print and iPad access

Institutional: £346 / US$646
print or online

Institutional: £433 / US$808
combined print and online

6-issue subscription
on Δ App for iPad:
£44.99 / US$64.99

Ray Winkler and Neil Spiller
would like to thank Eva
Menuhin for her dedicated
assistance in the preparation
of the manuscript of this
edition and the considerable
support of Simone Plekkepoel,
Lucy Davenport and Harriet
Portman from the STUFISH
studio in sourcing material.

MIX
Paper from
responsible sources
FSC
www.fsc.org FSC® C015829

ABOUT THE

GUEST–EDITOR AND EDITOR

RAY WINKLER AND NEIL SPILLER

Ray Winkler is a RIBA-registered UK architect, and CEO and Design Director of STUFISH Entertainment Architects. He began his design career as a carpenter and craftsman. He earned his Master's in Architecture from the Bartlett School of Architecture, University College London (UCL), and became interested in stage design and mobile architecture while undertaking postgraduate studies at the Southern California Institute of Architecture (SCI-Arc) in Los Angeles. He is drawn to the unique ephemeral and transformative nature of entertainment architecture and its emotional impact on audiences. He has devoted 25 years to designing live touring shows, theatrical projects, and spectacular one-off productions for a number of Summer and Winter Olympics, Commonwealth and Asian Games, and some of their respective handover ceremonies. He has also worked extensively on live TV shows for the BBC, MTV, VH1 and other channels in the US, Japan and UK, and with some of the biggest names in popular entertainment, including Beyoncé, Elton John, AC/DC, U2, the Rolling Stones, Robbie Williams, One Direction and Cirque du Soleil. Recent tours include Elton John's 'Farewell Yellow Brick Road' (2018–23), AC/DC's 'Rock or Bust' (2015–16), Arashi's live-stream only 'This Is ARASHI LIVE 2020.12.31' (2020), the Rolling Stones' 'No Filter' (2017–), and Beyoncé and Jay-Z's 'On the Run II' (2018).

Neil Spiller is Editor of 𝐷. He was previously Hawksmoor Chair of Architecture and Landscape and Deputy Pro Vice-Chancellor of the University of Greenwich, London. Prior to this he was Dean of its School of Architecture, Design and Construction and Professor of Architecture and Digital Theory, and before that Vice-Dean and Graduate Director of Design at the Bartlett, UCL. He has edited numerous 𝐷 issues, including 𝐷 *Celebrating the Marvellous* (2018) and the seminal 𝐷 *Architects in Cyberspace I and II* (1995 and 1998). His books include *Cyber Reader: Critical Writings for the Digital Era* (Phaidon, 2002), *Digital Dreams: The Architecture of the New Alchemic Technologies* (Watson-Guptill, 1998), *Visionary Architecture: Blueprints of the Modern Imagination* (Thames & Hudson, 2006) and *Surrealism and Architecture: A Blistering Romance* (Thames & Hudson, 2016). His architectural design work has been published and exhibited worldwide, and his drawings are held in many international collections. He is an internationally renowned visionary architect and his work has a remarkable graphic dexterity. He is also recognised for his paradigm-shifting contribution to architectural discourse, research/experiment and teaching. He has been a rock fan since the age of 11 when he first heard the LP *Deep Purple in Rock* (1970). 𝐷

Let Us Entertain You

A Glimpse Behind the Curtain

STUFISH,
ABBA Theatre,
London, 2021

Concept render. The portable theatre has been designed to house the ABBA Voyage show and immerse the 3,000-strong audience in the most spectacular audiovisual ABBA environment. The bespoke building can be fully demounted and transported to the next destination, setting a new benchmark for innovative shows and entertainment architecture.

From pharaohs, to princes, popes to pop stars, architecture has consistently been used as the catalyst to augment the power of performance. The desire for spectacle and its appropriate setting goes back millennia and architecture has been at the centre of its delivery. Whether it is the Pyramids of Giza, the agoras of ancient Greece, the Colosseum or the modern-day theatre, circus, arena or stadium, architecture has provided the envelope and backdrop for the unfolding performance. More particularly, it is entertainment architecture which provides the building blocks that create the event, trigger the emotions and embed the memories into our collective consciousness.

So, what exactly is 'entertainment architecture'? It is obviously nothing new, but has evolved since antiquity in line with technological developments and their utilisation of that technology by talented, lateral-thinking architects, designers and engineers. These creatives, some of whom are featured in this △, reveal the qualities that have given entertainment architecture such importance throughout the ages and, relatively recently, its centrality to contemporary society and our sense of self.

This issue of △ is about the current state of this design genre and how it was arrived at, using as a microcosm the varied and culturally significant work of STUFISH Entertainment Architects. Here, entertainment and architecture form a singularity that blurs the borders between the two to put emotions and the creation of memories at the epicentre of the experience.

An Ever-Changing Tradition

The suspension of disbelief and the imagined presence of the otherworldly, in the service of delight or transcendence, is crucial to entertainment architecture. Neil Spiller traces how the architects of the past have tried to achieve this magic and describes how digital representation, and the future of augmented reality, might change the ways audiences view and interact with performers and performances.

STUFISH,
Jean-Michel Jarre 'The Twelve
Dreams of the Sun' concert,
Giza, Egypt,
1999–2000

The stage for the performance was built half a kilometre in front of the Pyramids of Giza, so that they could be used as vast projection and lighting surfaces during the show, which began on the night of 31 December and carried on overnight to 1 January.

Before we get ahead of ourselves and speculate on the impact of augmented reality, it might serve us well to go back to the future of a more recent past when a powerful new way of forward thinking emerged out of the revolutionary haze and zeitgeist of that era.

In the 1960s and 1970s, progressive thinkers, painters and poets, pop stars and a handful of architects began to formalise a radical new way of thinking about the world in general and architecture in particular. Amongst them was the late Mark Fisher, who founded what was to become STUFISH in 1994. He developed a niche in the emerging world of touring music shows: rock and roll and architecture collided to create a bigger bang. Years later the echoes can still be heard, and after several permutations STUFISH has emerged as the clear leader in the field of entertainment architecture.

STUFISH,
Performance sphere,
Beijing Olympics,
Beijing,
2008

Sarah Brightman and Liu Huan performing You & Me at the top of the sphere. The sphere provided a versatile projection surface and the nine latitudinal rings, which were structural trusses, functioned as running tracks and performance areas 24 metres (80 feet) above the ground for up to 60 performers during the opening and closing.

The genre is sometimes criticised by the architectural profession as frivolous, too ephemeral and thus not really architecture. Such a view is strongly countered by the contributors to this *D* issue, beginning with Peter Cook, founder member of the influential 1960s group Archigram, who were interested in entertainment-based transient buildings. Cook argues that STUFISH's entertainment architecture is not only 'real' architecture, but a lineal descendant of the 'let's try it' culture of the Second World War's aeronautical engineers via the experimental, protean architecture of the 1970s–90s, and that STUFISH's consistent cross-disciplinary way of working foreshadowed the easy cross-cultural nature and intellectuality of today's younger generations.

This 'let's try it' culture underpins a fundamental approach to creativity at STUFISH. The slightly schizophrenic use and abuse of our left-brain/right-brain approach to problem solving allows STUFISH to cast its nets far and wide in the conviction that there are some big ideas out in the world that need to be captured and reeled in. This convergence of creativity, collaboration and curiosity creates the perfect storm in which ideas are tossed around and shaken up before the best ones emerge.

However, ideas never remain static and STUFISH's criteria of what makes some worthy of further investigation and development is ever evolving. The ecological impact the entertainment industry has on our world can no longer be ignored, nor should it be offered up as an inevitable and irresponsible by-product of a hedonistic fun-loving approach to architecture. So, in the spirit that regards problems merely as opportunities for solutions, STUFISH is actively involved with like-minded collaborators in trying to find ways in which we can minimise our footprint while still maximising our ability to stomp our feet to the beat of the world around us.

Neil Thomas of structural engineers Atelier One gives an insight in the issue into the dynamics of how this interdisciplinary collaboration between design and engineering, combined with inventiveness and the desire to investigate new ideas and technologies, has fuelled innovation in entertainment architecture, while speculating about how the ecological impact of touring shows might be reduced in the future.

Creating Thresholds of Liminality
Effective collaborative effort, in an atmosphere of respect and trust, is key to the process of creating the magic that is the essence of the emotional and narrative power of successful entertainment architecture. Writing in this issue, Aubrey Powell – film director, photographer, designer, and co-founder of the creatively multidimensional studio Hipgnosis – gives examples of how the potency of these narratives can pass into the real world and remain long after an entertainment event is history, while leading the reader through his collaboration with STUFISH for Pink Floyd and Monty Python.

Entertainment architecture creates the structures that allow the members of a tribe to focus their desires on the ultimate altars of entertainment – the stage and the theatre. Inspired designs emerge: steel trusses, fabric mesh and composite materials enveloped in video technology and peppered with hundreds of lights create intriguing architectural contexts in which shows unfold and buildings are constructed.

But what would form be without light, shape without colour, and music without emotions?

STUFISH,
Beyoncé 'Homecoming'
show, Coachella
Valley Music and
Arts Festival,
Indio,
California,
2018

Early concept sketch of Beyoncé's performance at Coachella, showing her and her dancers on the satellite stage amongst the crowd performing an elaborate choreography of scenery, lights and special effects.

STUFISH,
Skolkovo Black Box Theatre,
Moscow,
2014

Concept render. A high-tensile LED net
covers the twisting façade of this versatile,
multipurpose theatre housing a resident
show by Cirque du Soleil. The auditorium
space was designed with the flexibility to
accommodate a multitude of different event
configurations ranging from fashion shows
to product launches and music concerts.

In the hands of theatrical lighting designer Patrick Woodroffe, light takes on a dimension and plasticity that can be shaped. As his article demonstrates, in his collaborations with STUFISH, the transformative nature of light becomes an end in itself. Integrating scenic design, architecture and lighting results in a hybrid form of design where it is difficult to tell where one begins and the other ends.

Memories are the currency in which we trade our experiences with our tribe to generate the connections needed by our desire to belong. Over the centuries, the physical world has been there to provide us with this context. This may be about to change as virtual experiences are becoming ever more immersive, compelling and accessible. Extended-reality and digital interactive performance expert Ash Nehru's article makes the case that augmented and virtual reality will soon be able not only to create the spectacle, but also to deliver the group intimacy and the connections between performers and fans that audiences truly crave.

Coupled with this train of thought, social anthropologist Haidy Geismar goes on to explore how social media are shifting the experience of the crowd at mass entertainment events. The singular moment of 'being there' has become an embodied experience dispersed across time and space, shared by millions of users and prolonged in an ongoing and participatory curation of both public and private memory.

'The Instagram moment' now defines not only how we experience the event, but how we design for it. Captured by millions of mobile phones, the un-curated display of design across the digital universe has made all artists acutely aware of how the medium through which we practise our art and publish our designs creates the feedback loop between entertainment and architecture. All that is solid melts into the ether.

Design and Memory

We do, however, design things that are built in the physical realm, and that process is as intricate as it is intriguing. In the secure knowledge that time waits for no one (or so the song goes), STUFISH's trusted collaborators in the world of entertainment architecture, manufacture and fabrication make things happen at speed in situations where most people in the conventional construction industry would be paralysed when faced with the pace and complexity with which this needs to happen.

In his article in this $\mathcal{D}$ issue, Adam Davis – Chief Creative Officer of architectural engineering and software company TAIT – explains TAIT's 'design spiral' approach to creating the spectacles that world-class modern live events demand. They achieve results within very restricted timeframes using a unique cross-disciplinary, collaborative process of concurrent design and manufacturing, embracing the design dead-ends and the experimentation that come with repeated prototyping.

At the other end of entertainment architecture's spectrum lie some of the more permanent examples of STUFISH's work.

When designing themed and purpose-built theatres, the challenge is to go beyond the existing technology to support the unique vision of the specific production. Writing here, performance environment specialist S. Leonard Auerbach describes the pathway of development for such architectural projects, and how advances in theatrical technology are enabling the industry to create architectural environments that respond to unlimited artistic expression.

Riffing off this interesting line of thought and jumping between STUFISH's permanent and temporary designs, STUFISH partner MAciej Woroniecki explains the complex architectural design requirements and creative processes behind the development and narrative-driven design of successful auditoriums and theatres. He also details the additional challenges posed by creating stages for touring shows, which must function both within their own confines and the constraints of various venues, while being efficient to transport, set up and take down.

STUFISH,
UAE 40th National Day Celebrations,
Zayed Sports City Stadium,
Abu Dhabi,
2012

The 40-metre (130-foot) tall structure in the centre of Abu Dhabi's Zayed Sports City Stadium stood on a 9-metre (30-foot) tall plinth, and provided over 6,000 square metres (65,000 square feet) of projection surface. The plinth housed substage storage and dressing rooms for cast and props that gained stage access via large barn doors and mechanical lifts. Four 3-metre (10-foot) wide steel portals were used for performer flying, lighting and projection positions.

There is no civilisation that does not have entertainment at the core of its cultural offerings, and one need not be a neuroscientist to know that we humans are tribal by nature and hard-wired to collectively seek pleasure in one form or another. The need for 'bread and circuses' has found its way into the 21st century to provide new ways to entertain, aspire, desire and dream our way out of our often-dreary everyday routine.

One of the catalysts for this emotive experience is music. It is inextricably linked with our personal autobiography, and the experience of music is intrinsically coupled with the experience of the physical environment in which it happens. Architect and academic Robert Kronenburg explains in his article how entertainment architects design immersive events which combine spectacle and fantasy to create moments that the audience will remember and reflect on for the rest of their lives.

A momentary lapse of reason is probably what brought STUFISH into the realm of exhibition design. Navigating between the artefacts and architecture of exhibitions, STUFISH embarked on an interesting journey of discovery that began many years ago when Pink Floyd grasped the importance of narrative designs for their great gigs and sought the help of architecture to deliver their spectacle on a grand scale.

Curator and exhibition maker Victoria Broackes's article tells the story behind 'Pink Floyd: Their Mortal Remains' – one of the most successful exhibitions ever to have been staged at London's Victoria and Albert Museum. STUFISH and Aubrey Powell designed a spectacular theatrical environment in the temporary space of the display that distilled and evoked the experience of Pink Floyd's music and concerts, placing it alongside objects, costumes and artefacts illustrating the band's cultural impact.

While Willie Williams – show director, stage and lighting designer, video and set designer for concerts, theatre and multimedia projects – here muses, in an interview with STUFISH partner Ric Lipson, on the changes, both good and bad, that advances in technology have brought to entertainment design,

STUFISH,
Han Show,
Han Show Theatre,
Wuhan, China,
2014

Early concept sketch exploring robot arms and their LED screens interfacing with physical props and performers to create an intricate choreography between the digital and physical world.

STUFISH,
Concept design proposal
for 'We Meet Again'
post-pandemic
Thames River show,
London,
2020

The concept illustrated is for a
floating stage in front of Tower Bridge.
The stage consists of a series of
floating barges with mechanical arms
and telescoping towers that would
hold all the equipment necessary to
stage a spectacular show celebrating
the end of the Covid-19 worldwide
pandemic.

e acknowledges that technology – and especially he mobile phone – has created a new reality for live ntertainment. The once-ephemeral experience of a how is now curated, shared and memorialised by the udience, raising the question of where the ultimate ct of creation now lies.

When designing stage sets, the audience perspective nd experience is often taken as the vantage point rom which the concept and creative process find their ractical application. While making sure that the set ooks fabulous, audience sightlines are not obstructed nd video screens are large enough for even the most emote audience member to see their favourite artist, ne can easily forget the reverse perspective that the rtist has of the show and the audience watching it. Vhat is it like to occupy this space and deliver the erformance of a lifetime that will leave indelible nemories in the minds of the fans?

In a rare interview with Queen's Brian May and Roger aylor, the members of the legendary band describe the nique relationship between the artist and the audience, nd how their now iconic stage designs, developed with TUFISH over the years, became an extension of their nusic and their performance.

Having woven together the interesting insights, houghts and narratives of our collaborators to ssemble a rich tapestry of images, renders, models, iagrams and sketches, it is hoped that this edition of Δ ill give the reader a glimpse into the weirdly wonderful nd creative world of STUFISH, and entertainment rchitecture as a whole.

It only remains for you to join me, our collaborators, y fellow STUFISH partners Alicia Tkacz, MAciej Voroniecki, Ric Lipson, Simone Plekkepoel and ur fellow STUFISHERs, and to sit back and let us ntertain you. Δ

When designing stage sets, the audience perspective and experience is often taken as the vantage point from which the concept and creative process find their practical application

STUFISH,
'We Meet Again' post-pandemic Thames River show,
London,
2020

Concept render overview at night showing the various set pieces
along the river. The performance uses the city, the river, its bridges
and embankment as both stage and auditorium.

6

STUFISH
ENTERTAINMENT ARCHITECTS

DESIGNING SENSORY

JS PLEASURE

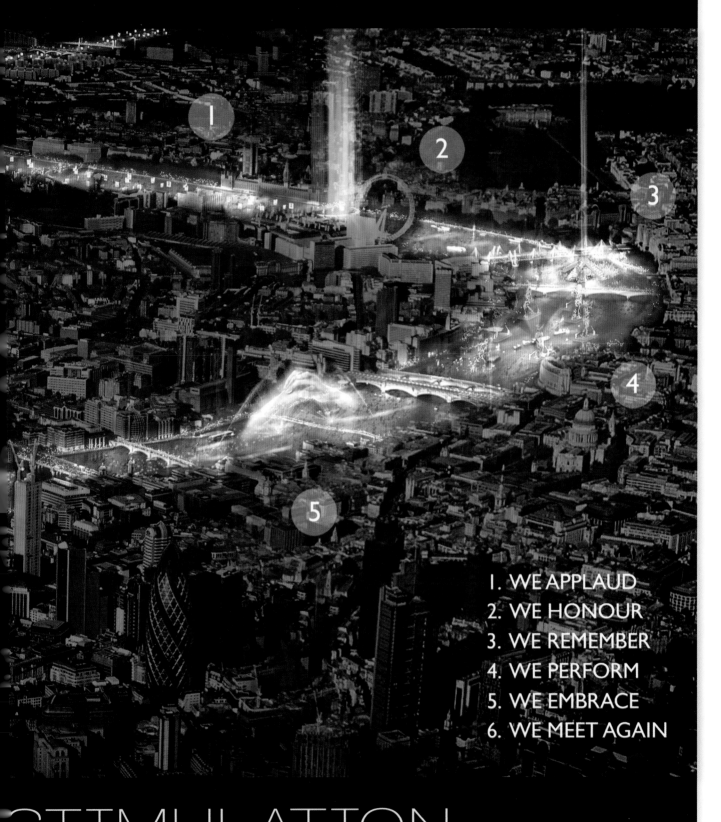

1. WE APPLAUD
2. WE HONOUR
3. WE REMEMBER
4. WE PERFORM
5. WE EMBRACE
6. WE MEET AGAIN

STIMULATION

Designing architecture has always been about creating and conducting spatial experiences. Likewise this choreography of space, points of view, vistas and the unfolding of performative narratives through materiality and time are all critical components of entertainment architecture. ⊿'s Editor **Neil Spiller** explores how the work of STUFISH resonates with and further amplifies familiar themes across architecture's history.

Andrea Pozzo,
Church of St Ignatius of
Loyola at Campus Martius,
Rome,
after 1685

The ceiling of the church features a painted anamorphic perspective dome that appears real from certain viewpoints. This early use of illusion for theatrical effect gives the building a more majestic presence.

In a world where architects are prone to a lot of soul-searching and worthy guilt about the state of the world and the destinies of its populations, and have a hubris about their role in being able to mitigate these inequalities, it is joyous to be writing about a celebration of sensory stimulation and creative fun.

'Entertainment architecture' nowadays is a continuum, a spectrum, if you like, of a myriad of possible points in between architecture and entertainment. The genetics of a show is a synthesis of various types of mechanics – structural, electronic and performative. The technologies that enable these combinations can range from the normatively simple to the hugely complicated, and are often reappropriated from other disciplines and uses. A good example of this synthesis of high- and low-tech is the façade of STUFISH's Han Show Theatre (known as the 'Red Lantern') in Wuhan (2014), China, which deliberately uses over 17,000 red discs to create a low-res dot-matrix screen when normally architecture and urban centres strive for high-res options without much thought.

Magic and the Imagination

British science-fiction writer Arthur C Clarke's famous and often cited Third Law states: 'Any sufficiently advanced technology is indistinguishable from magic.'[1] It is this sense, this suspension of disbelief and the imagined presence of the otherworldly, that is crucial to entertainment architecture. Trying to achieve this magic has permeated the history of architecture and entertainment.

Filippo Brunelleschi's development of architectural perspectives from the 15th century enabled artists to create *trompe-l'oeil* frescoes of imagined spaces within buildings and then subsequently to toy with the rules of perspective. An example is Andrea Pozzo's beautiful illusionist frescoes within the interior of the Church of St Ignatius of Loyola at Campus Martius in Rome (after 1685) with its painted 'dome' that fools the eye into believing it is real.

Other notable works include Andrea Palladio and Vincenzo Scamozzi's Teatro Olimpico in Vicenza (1585) with its *trompe-l'oeil* stage backdrop giving the illusion of its streets stretching into the distance when seen by the audience through the Roman-styled *scaenae frons*. It is the oldest stage set that survives.

Following this line of development was English architect Inigo Jones, who designed sets and costumes for the delectation of the Stuart royal court. These extravagant performances, known as masques and often penned by the playwright and poet Ben Jonson, included elaborate scenery and players in expensive bespoke finery. In bringing the masques to the stage, Jones thus made a significant contribution to the development of entertainment design. He was the first in Britain to use movable scenery and the proscenium arch.

The interplay between the virtual and the real in architecture for the benefit of performance has been played out over centuries. Churches and cathedrals,

STUFISH,
Han Show Theatre,
Wuhan, China, 2014

Here STUFISH opted for a low-resolution approach using 17,000 red discs.

Andrea Palladio and Vincenzo Scamozzi,
Teatro Olimpico,
Vicenza, Italy,
1585

This *trompe-l'oeil* stage backdrop uses distorted perspective to give the impression of receding streets and alleyways disappearing into the distance when seen from the audience.

for example, are in effect immersive stage sets for communal rituals led by the clergy, who interact with the symbols/icons of their history and worldview while reciting their poetic liturgy. Tricks and props were developed like statues of saints weeping or bleeding to add to the theatre of it all. Stained-glass windows project divine light into a rainbow of colours depicting images telling stories that illustrate the scriptures. Cathedrals were particularly designed to bring you to your knees in humble worship and convince of a higher, magical power.

Touching the Ground Lightly

Whilst Jones's sets, Pozzo's frescoes and the Teatro Olimpico use classical architectural motifs, and the cathedral the classical but often the Gothic lexicon, STUFISH's designs have no overriding architectural style – everything is designed from the bottom-up. Whilst Jones's various masques were performed around 500 times and required quick erection and the swift striking of scenery, STUFISH's projects have a considerably wider reach than these predecessors, and are seen around the world in person, on YouTube or any screen near you. But whatever the production, it has two imperatives. Firstly, to leave no trace – the same design has to be built in different places around the world 50 to 100 times as a global tour progresses. Detail, transience, expediency and the resilience and robustness of constituent elements is crucial. Secondly, but even more importantly, is for the production to talk to the emotions and create a visceral excitement when in use – to be a machine for creating memories. STUFISH's work is designed to provoke an attitude of gay abandon in the audience and a sense of intimacy. Their work often attempts to deconstruct the invisible 'fourth wall' between act and viewer, using walkways and movable stages penetrating deep into the crowd, huge electronic screens not just at the back of the stage but again, deep within the audience. So much for Jones's proscenium now!

This elimination of the fourth wall can also be extrapolated as negating the boundaries between the act and architecture. STUFISH's Dai Show Theatre in Xishuangbanna, China (2015) is an example. The building, its low ceiling and its structure became part of the scenery (featured on the cover image on this *Ɒ* issue),

Reality Augmented

Augmented reality (AR) is provoking new ways to view performances and interact with them, and can create a new and manipulatable closeness to the artists. Our highly dexterous computer-enabled spaces and performances of today not only further expand this historical lexicon of techniques of architectural illusion, but offer the opportunity to design new types of performative spaces that are both real, virtual and dynamically capable of being navigated and created in real time. Peter Zellner, writing in 1999, speculated on the impact these technologies might therefore instigate:

STUFISH,
Robbie Williams
'Take The Crown' tour,
O2 Arena, London,
2013

The power of the ecclesiastical stage-setting and the light through stained glass still resonates in today's more secular performances.

It is, perhaps, instructive to seek to find parallels between the dynamics of art history and the evolution of digital space to try to establish how entertainment architecture might evolve in the coming years in relation to these technologies architecture capable of addressing – or better yet, choreographing – the dance between the doubled worlds of the real-actual and the virtual-potential is beginning to present itself.'[2] Whilst such ideas have been relatively common currency for the last 20 or so years, it is only recently that these technologies have been sufficiently developed and cheap enough for frequent architectural and theatrical experimentation. It is, perhaps, instructive to seek to find parallels between the dynamics of art history and the evolution of digital space to try to establish how entertainment architecture might evolve in the coming years in relation to these technologies. From the time Brunelleschi perfected perspective, and its subsequent development through innovations in the number of vanishing points and varying points of view creating representations that better simulated our anthropocentric way of seeing, to the Modernist period that began to establish itself in *fin-de-siècle* and early-20th-century Paris, for example, perspective became foreshortened, fragmented and even subjugated totally in favour of different points of view on one canvas depicting objects in motion. Modernist art became imbued with changing durations, ways of seeing and speed – in effect the 'choreography' Zellner alludes to in relation to the architectures of the virtually real. What might these parallels teach us about the next steps of digital representation and the future of AR in

relation to entertainment architecture? In considering the ramifications of augmented reality, an amazing array of concepts emerges. In augmented reality the city is mostly empty – a blank canvas on which to transcribe architectures, responsive to individual points of view, at varying scales and at varying times and durations. Zellner, in the same 1999 essay, alludes to these potentialities: 'These experimental forms promise to occupy the coterminous territories of the real and the virtual. In them we may begin to experience a world no longer divided by virtuality but one made rich with spaces of animated potentials and realities.'[3] You could project yourself onto the stage with the players – the possibilities are endless. Continuing and exponential AR dexterity in the digital world will afford designers and artists the possibility of radically redesigning the relationship between audience and performer as well as performance and architecture, and STUFISH has already begun this journey.

STUFISH,
Han Show Theatre,
Wuhan, China,
2014

The LED screens from within the theatre are on giant arms that move around, helping to animate shows and break down the divide between audience and performers.

Pandemic Silver Linings

The recent lockdowns and live-performance lay-offs have provoked STUFISH into using their huge capacity for experimentation and innovation to muse and project ideas about the future of their profession – a silver lining of the global pandemic cloud and viral shutdown of their industry. Two projects in particular come to mind, one more poignant than the other and context specific, the other much more multivalent, but both highly transient.

Vertical Theatre Group,
Vertical Theatre,
2021

Opposite: Concept render of the exterior showing the theatre's colourful, well-ventilated façade and transient, reconfigurable construction.

Below: Render of the interior illustrating a performance in progress. The Vertical Theatre is designed as an intimate, travelling venue that disappears without a trace when the show is over.

'We Meet Again' (2020) is posited for a near-future time where Covid-19 has been vanquished. It takes its initial inspiration from London's Thames River pageant tradition where processions of boats progress up or down the river to celebrate historical events, the last one in 2012 for the Queen's Diamond Jubilee. It consists of six elements. 'We Applaud' has 200 floating video screens starting at Hampton Court and finishing at Parliament and St Thomas's Hospital. The screens show the faces of firefighters, soldiers and NHS personnel, culminating in a ritual public applause. 'We Honour' is a rainbow light installation centred on Westminster Bridge to celebrate our enhanced community spirit through lockdown, and 'We Remember' a choir raised above the river with floating, dissolving candles – a time for remembrance. At the South Bank, 'We Perform' is a series of large, lit floating barges of giant sculptures of performers of all sorts. 'We Embrace', along Hungerford Bridge, is formed by a mist within which can be seen two hands holding, and finally 'We Meet Again' is a circular stage at Tower Bridge with live performance and a halo of flying drones to create the light show. STUFISH have consciously enlarged this entertainment architecture to an urban scale where the river is the stage and the city is the audience.

STUFISH are also part of the Vertical Theatre Group, which has been grappling with the idea of how to design a tourable performance space – the Vertical Theatre (2021) – a complete demountable building that can operate in a pandemic or post-pandemic world, one that creates a new intimacy for the audience with the performers, can accommodate a variety of stage shows, is responsive to whatever regime of social distancing/bubbling or not as the case may be in the future, and leaves its site with no trace. Numerous vertical theatres could tour the world, reinvigorating the ailing live entertainment industry. It has a capacity of 1,200 to 2,400 people.

STUFISH continue to innovate even in unprecedented times and their resilience, ambition and diligence results in extraordinary structures and events. Their future is indeed bright as they complete their first quarter of a century. There is much to be done and many discoveries to be made for billions of people's sheer frivolous pleasure. ⚡

Notes
1. Arthur C Clarke, 'Hazards of Prophecy: The Failure of the Imagination' [1962], in *Profiles of the Future: An Inquiry into the Limits of the Possible,* Orion (London), 1973, p 14.
2. Peter Zellner, *Hybrid Space: New Forms in Digital Architecture,* Thames & Hudson (London and New York), 1999, p 11.
3. *Ibid.*

Peter Cook

BACK TO
THE FUTURE:

THE ARCHITECTURE OF ENTERTAINMENT

Throughout **Peter Cook**'s long and influential career, he has been at the epicentre of architectural education and architectural speculation. Here he remembers some of the genesis moments of entertainment architecture and its characters. Using examples from STUFISH's oeuvre he asserts that entertainment architecture is Architecture with a capital 'A' and at least as relevant as any of the discipline's other manifestations.

STUFISH,
Han Show Theatre,
Wuhan, China,
2014

The theatre's shape references a traditional Chinese paper lantern, its surface suggested by fine cable nets tensioned between eight intersecting steel rings, suspended around the fly tower. At the net's 18,000 nodes, red aluminium disks support LEDs. At night, the façade seems to be created of light, dematerialising the building's substance. Slender support columns represent the lantern's tassels, and the podium roof profile evokes the curving profile of traditional Chinese roofs.

When recalling the various phases of the Architectural Association (AA) School of Architecture's development, the early 1970s evokes a big smile. That was when a definitively upbeat and stylish set of characters appeared and somehow vaulted over the worthy, denim-clad, well-meaning characters that had just preceded them. This cohort of ebullient individuals were not afraid to indulge in 'escape' and articulate their imagination, often through such personalities as Piers Gough – who today retains his sharp wit and naughty eye, or Janet Bull – who became the media personality Janet Street-Porter and thus the quotable mirror of the period.

Amongst them, however, lurked a subset who nurtured parallel enthusiasms for invention and relished the process of investigation, yet without the remotest hint of nerdiness – this was the AA after all, where obsession was considered uncool. They were excited about robots, gadgets and vehicles – with which Andrew Holmes, decades later, continues to delight through his unbelievably 'real' depictions of auto-Americana. Best of all, though, was the tangible delight of the inflatable. To make a 'blow-up' in the garden, pipe in some air from your vacuum cleaner (and then probably watch it slowly leak) was a statement of faith.

STUFISH,
AC/DC 'Rock or Bust' world tour,
Arnhem, The Netherlands,
2015

Rosie is linked to the AC/DC song 'Whole Lotta Rosie'. Here shown on site in Arnhem, the inflatable, fabricated by Airworks Amsterdam, is approximately 10 metres (33 feet) wide by 6 metres (20 feet) tall, and is used as a stage prop during AC/DC's touring shows, appearing when her eponymous song is played.

STUFISH,
Chimelong Theatre,
Hengqin Island,
Zhuhai, China,
2019

The 6,700-bespoke-seat theatre's undulating, rippling façade echoes the iconic form of the circus tent and the fluid quality of the folds of stage curtains, although its permanent structure can withstand the area's seasonal typhoons. Gold is the predominant colour, but red and blue, also iconic circus colours, are incorporated into the façade, creating a kind of static motion as the viewer's angle of vision changes.

An explosion –
sometimes literally
– had taken place in
the world of optics,
electrics and digital
technology. Yet in
architecture, the
business of building
was still mostly slow,
messy and heavy

One of the subset was quietly making far more of it than that: the late Mark Fisher, future founder of STUFISH, who graduated from the AA in 1971 and became a Unit Master 1973–7. He was intelligent enough to realise that the pure inflatable was not an end in itself, but a possible component that could be added to the growing arsenal of invention along with the robots and the gadgets. He began to weave the cranky, metallic parts together with the pulsating inflatables to form hybrids that moved but could not really be categorised.

A mental jump of 20 years, to the Bartlett School of Architecture, University College London, in the mid-1990s, evokes another wide smile at memories of the marvellous phase when, propelled by a substantial importation of AA talent as my 'team', we had taken the fusty old Bartlett by the scruff of the neck and got it rolling with a real spirit of invention and imagination zazzing around the old place. The notion of 'armature' was on everyone's lips and erupted into bat-like, skeleton-like, tent-like creations, so that in the jury of a Final Year project the lives of Christine Hawley, CJ Lim, myself and the outside critics were literally threatened by a flying bomb that whizzed round above our heads. But we need not have worried (perhaps) as the author was one Ray Winkler, known for his inventiveness and having returned from SCI-Arc (Southern California Institute of Architecture) as a worthy ambassador of the Bartlett 'thing'. If ever it can be said to have done so, the school had escaped from the long arm of prosaic British architecture.

By the 1990s, these two generations of inventive architects and advocates of the 'let's try it' culture could carry over essential references dating back more than forty years: including Barnes Neville Wallis's invention of the bouncing bomb (1942) used in the 'Dambusters' raid during the Second World War (16–17 May 1943) and the almost indestructible geodetic lamella framework of the Wellington bomber (mid-1930s), and Richard Buckminster Fuller's challenge of the architectural tradition of mass, staticity and weight. An explosion – sometimes literally – had taken place in the world of optics, electrics and digital technology. Yet in architecture, despite the fact that most experimental architects had been teaching, especially in the three above-mentioned schools, the business of building was still mostly slow, messy and heavy.

Early Days

In 1977, already a seasoned young teacher at the AA, Mark Fisher was able to return to old preoccupations with structures capable of undergoing morphological and transmissive changes in response to external signals with his Responsive Dwelling project (RDP), which was a hybrid inflatable made from hexagonal cells that could change in size and transparency. There were complex valve systems and membranes that regulated energy transmission and allowed solar gain to be controlled at the outer surface. He built prototypes and his work began to appear in architectural and design biennales. However it was in his amazing airbrush drawing of the Responsive Dwelling project that he communicated something else; it is a delight in the stylish, dreamlike, almost otherworldly potential of the gadgetry. Without knowing the blow-by-blow history of exactly how Fisher came to work on the settings for music experiences, I am convinced that he saw in them both a reality in which he could invent 'stuff' as well as a challenge to step further into the experiential unknown. Similarly musicians saw in him the means to catapult an audience into a delirium beyond the merely aural – as if the most exotic album sleeves of that time were able to leap off the page into the sky.

At first Fisher worked in partnership with Jonathan Park, a structural engineer who also taught at the AA. Then, working almost continuously with structural engineers Atelier One and in particular with the mercurial genius of Neil Thomas, the duo realised that in the world of rock and roll everything had to rock – for sure – but that the way it rolled needed to be safe, quick, feasible and repeatable. The history of STUFISH that grew from this liaison is not only the exponential product of its inventiveness but part of its family history. It happened that Ray Winkler was working at Atelier One as a student and therefore following all of this. When the time came for his final external examination, in the 1990s at the Bartlett, the examiner was – intriguingly – one Mark Fisher.

It was not the first or last time that a student would crawl out of the event reporting that Mark had given him or her a real grilling and a run of piercing criticism, which would later contrast with Mark's own comment to us over lunch that the scheme had been brilliant. So with Ray. Three weeks later Mark offered him a job and, unwittingly, set him onto the path of eventual succession at STUFISH.

Before delving a little more into the evolution of projects, one must continue to ponder on the context, for all this was happening in parallel to the British High Tech world and the emerging international digital roll-over, as well as in a more local context where experimentation in the realm of built buildings was imperceptibly moving towards another period of conservatism. Students and interns were lucky if they could work for Will Alsop, Future Systems or Ian Ritchie, who were still fighting and experimenting in London, or for Coop Himmelb(l)au in Vienna, but for most kids it was a question of quietly burying foolish dreams of 'another' architecture.

Spirits of Place

Yet a giant pig could fly in the sky, and contraptions that would have been considered impossibly far-fetched, at least at any of the 'crits' that I have sat on in any of the three aforementioned schools, have actually been constructed – disappearing after the show into dozens of natty crates and trolleys, but effectively living out the scenario that I had tentatively drawn in the Instant City (1968–70). This cannot but provoke one into asking 'Why isn't more architecture like that? Is it only allowed to happen in the world of entertainment?' This question has become oddly piquant since I have been able to watch my own music producer son, Alexander (AG) Cook, working with venues, makers, craftspeople, artistes, graphic designers, video artists and a wide and heterogeneous cast of other characters, some of whom combine these skills. From this I observe that photographic imagery – stretched and made more evanescent in every conceivable way – is the increasingly preferred territory against which the music is heard, and it seems to be at the core of recent work by STUFISH.

Poor landlocked architects might sometimes play with pastiche, may delve into virtual reality but seem to shy away from the deliberate distortion of reality that is no longer tied to referential reality. Many of our generation dreamed that architecture could be stretched, move, disappear, metamorphose – but generally it did not. Even so, we rarely wished to distort it out of any reference to known environment or territory. Of course the clue was already there, way back when Fisher called his AA Unit the 'Nice Ideas Unit'. Nice ideas do not need to be consistent.

So I watch STUFISH move in and out of what might be called 'located sets' rather than architecture. If in the same space the Rolling Stones can be both larger than life and as small as a real group of guys making a noise on a platform, and if any context/image/distortion/mirage can be coincident with the sound, then the characteristics of the place to which your attention is being drawn – that 'spot', 'patch', 'zone', 'focus' – are significant at *that moment*. The territory in which it is convenient to enjoy this may be a seat, a terrace, a headset, a sofa. Tradition evolved the theatre but then came the drive-in, where you opted into and out of the event. At the time of writing,

STUFISH is working on a Covid-safe theatre, the Vertical Theatre, which is very loose and light – a spiral of 'opera-boxes', and almost a will-o'-the-wisp since it is moveable. Their performance sets have gone far, far beyond my Archigram colleague Ron Herron's lovely projects Sets Fit for the Queen (1974) or Suburban Sets (1975). They invoke smoke and electronics and endless supplies of pressurised air and, again, the images of faces or bodies that are as large as a cloud – if so wished.

Yet, intriguingly, one senses something more than a circumstantial attachment to the mechanical. Of course Madonna needs to prance around; Beyoncé needs to stretch her arms and legs; Lady Gaga to be operationally as gaga as she can. That involves surface, weight, vibration, and that pesky business of dismantling and constructing the set absolutely reliably time and again over the course of months – but quickly! Trusses and bolted-together technology offer the most logical solution. Valves, cushions, hawsers and drifting drapes are sometimes dodgier. Metal has good associations too – back to the wartime boffins, via all those engineering conversations.

Poor landlocked architects might sometimes play with pastiche, may delve into virtual reality but seem to shy away from the deliberate distortion of reality that is no longer tied to referential reality

STUFISH,
The Rolling Stones 'No Filter' tour,
Europe and North America,
2017–

Hand sketch. The band wanted a sleek, modern look for this tour. This was achieved with four 22-metre (72-foot) monolithic LED screen towers which hid all the technical components. The band played under a custom-built roof, and all lighting fixtures were integrated into the structures, further enhancing the stage set's elegant simplicity.

Synthesis and Metamorphosis

Primitive parallels to what STUFISH does are the visiting circuses or fairgrounds of the past, although no one would ever have considered them to have anything to do with day-to-day experience. Yet the accumulated devices, technique, experiments and general know-how that STUFISH wield in their creations could now – if we had the nerve – be added to the architectural canon. Why shouldn't part of a Westfield shopping centre erupt in-and-out of a developed version of their Han Show Theatre in Wuhan (2014, known as 'the Red Lantern') but then reconstitute itself as a photographic explosion in the sky? Why shouldn't a garden turn into a gyrating stage? Before going completely off-piste I could, of course, list all the tricks that the early Mark Fisher through to present-day STUFISH have accumulated. I could point to their ingenuity in creating everything from carbon-fibre trees to pictures-onto-pixels.

I could suggest too, that such an approach resonates exactly with the letter, as well as the spirit, of such weird craft as the tiny but versatile Westland Lysander aeroplane (Arthur Davenport and 'Teddy' Potter, 1936) or the Bailey bridges of the Second World War (Donald Bailey, 1940–41). These were almost more gadgets than proper 'things'.

STUFISH,
Stage design,
Commonwealth Games,
Delhi,
2010

There was no room or capacity to hang the technical hardware required for a big outdoor show at Delhi's Jawaharlal Nehru Stadium (Gerkan, Marg & Partners, 2010). STUFISH's huge, floating aerostat was the solution. It provided a 360-degree projection surface and became the unique signature of the show, which depicted various aspects of Indian life and history and blended art and technology into a single entity.

STUFISH,
Wuhan Movie Theme Park,
Wuhan, China,
2014

above: The entirely self-contained theme park's bell-like structures reference the historically and culturally important set of similarly shaped 2,400-year-old bronze bianzhong chime bells housed in the Hubei Provincial Museum, Wuhan, and are arranged in a way which implies the bells are ringing – creating a kind of static dynamism that expresses an almost audible clangour.

below: Animated LED discs line the Grand Atrium's inner façade. They create an interactive digital platform displaying vibrant choreographed theatrical lighting that enhances the multi-dimensional energy of the architecture. The fully contained complex houses retail and restaurant spaces, 4K and 5K resolution cinema screens, a flight theatre and other film-related 'ride' attractions.

STUFISH have kept in touch with the upcoming generation – occasionally through teaching but immeasurably more often by inspiring, while amusing and entertaining them

STUFISH,
Nanchang Wanda Mall,
Nanchang, China,
2016

The concept for the façade is inspired by the world-famous Chinese blue-and-white porcelain, produced for over 1,000 years in the local town of Jingdezhen, Jiangxi province. The large curving three-dimensional forms of the façade break up the plaza's volume into smaller, human-scale street frontages, and are clad in large blue-and-white porcelain tiles, in characteristic floral and fantasy patterns.

Those who might dismiss such a train of thought as irrelevant, saying that STUFISH design for events, and that only solid buildings are architecture, while gatekeeping the definition of what constitutes a 'legitimate' trajectory of architecture along with a 'legitimate' language and a system of parts, should beware. Not only have STUFISH, Atelier One, their friends and allies pulled in some of the smartest brains in the profession, they have kept in touch with the upcoming generation – occasionally through teaching but immeasurably more often by inspiring, while amusing and entertaining them. My convictions in this regard have been reinforced by listening to the dinner-table conversations of my son's music cronies (on the occasions that mum and dad were allowed to be party to them).

Possibly they might be part of a certain circuit, but the old 1960s idea of the music scene being made up of people lacking intelligence is completely knocked on the head by the fact that virtually all of them are graduates

– often of arcane disciplines such as Russian literature. They discuss their craft and gossip, as do we all, but they have an intriguing ability to overlay many different references or conditioners, jumping from Mozart to soft focus, to pedal distortion, to the atmosphere of Oakland, California in one sentence. Their conversation reflects that same witty, febrile, immensely cultured stream that STUFISH is part of – jumping from dream and distortion, to double-image, to geometric drift, to romantic reference, to 'look no hands' engineering in one move.

They are cultured in the sense that their world and conversation and creations absorb and synthesise many, many phenomena, whereas my memory of the old architectural 'scene' of my early years is that it tried to capture one culture and hang on to it.

STUFISH is most certainly architecture! ᴓ

INNOV
THINKI

ENGINEERING
SOLUTIONS

Atelier One for STUFISH design,
Structural isometric view,
U2 '360°' world tour,
2009–11

Seven to eight days were required to assemble and dismantle
'The Claw' using high-pressure, state-of-the art hydraulic
systems. As the time between performances was less than
that, three identical sets were built. One would be in use, the
second being assembled at the next venue, and the third, at the
previous venue, in the process of being dismantled.

ISOMETRIC VIEW

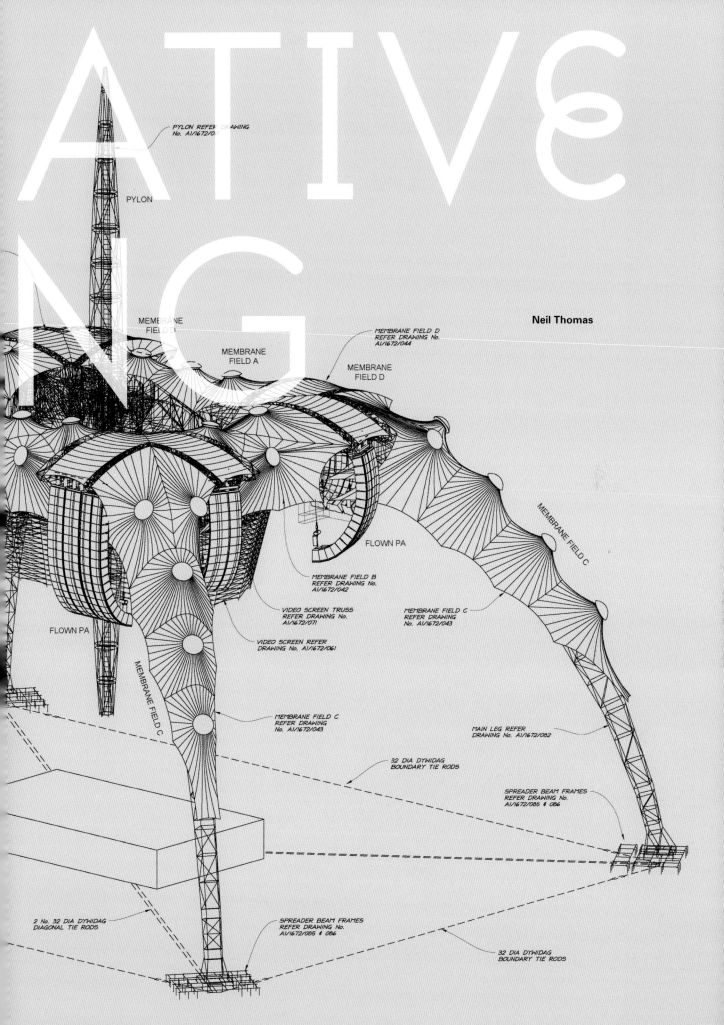

ATIVε
NG

Neil Thomas

PYLON REFER DRAWING
No. AI/1672/0?!

PYLON

MEMBRANE
FIELD D

MEMBRANE
FIELD A

MEMBRANE FIELD D
REFER DRAWING No.
AI/1672/044

MEMBRANE
FIELD D

MEMBRANE FIELD C

FLOWN PA

MEMBRANE FIELD B
REFER DRAWING No.
AI/1672/042

VIDEO SCREEN TRUSS
REFER DRAWING No.
AI/1672/071

MEMBRANE FIELD C
REFER DRAWING
No. AI/1672/043

FLOWN PA

VIDEO SCREEN REFER
DRAWING No. AI/1672/061

MEMBRANE FIELD C

MEMBRANE FIELD C
REFER DRAWING
No. AI/1672/043

MAIN LEG REFER
DRAWING No. AI/1672/082

32 DIA DYWIDAG
BOUNDARY TIE RODS

SPREADER BEAM FRAMES
REFER DRAWING No.
AI/1672/085 & 086.

2 No. 32 DIA DYWIDAG
DIAGONAL TIE RODS

SPREADER BEAM FRAMES
REFER DRAWING No.
AI/1672/085 & 086.

32 DIA DYWIDAG
BOUNDARY TIE RODS

NEIL THOMAS, founder of structural engineering firm Atelier One, has had an enduring and symbiotic relationship with STUFISH. He and his team have played a key part in designing the structures of some of the most audacious stage shows and rock gigs in recent years. He recounts how those stages, which have an iconic presence in the history of contemporary music, came about.

Consistent and successful innovation requires both the ability to imagine new ideas, and the willingness to collaborate with others to bring these ideas to fruition. The STUFISH team have surrounded themselves with collaborators throughout their long and inspiring history as entertainment architects. For over 25 years the structural engineering firm Atelier One, specialising in lightweight portable architecture, has been one of those close collaborators, allowing both organisations to offer an insight into the dynamics of how interdisciplinary collaboration between design and engineering, combined with inventiveness and the desire to investigate new ideas and technologies, can fuel innovation.

LED Screens

The development of the first full-size, full-colour outdoor touring LED screen used during U2's 'PopMart' world tour (1997–8) revolutionised the industry.

The introduction of a commercially available blue LED in the early 1990s had made full-colour LED displays possible, and several companies were beginning to produce them in the late 1990s. Large-scale video screens already existed but touring them was difficult: they were heavy and bulky; and maintaining power and data connections, so the screen could be installed quickly and reliably at a new venue every few days for over a year, was an issue.

Mark Fisher and his STUFISH studio realised that the pixels could be spaced further apart to achieve larger images, especially at night, because audiences would be viewing the screens from long distances. This made it possible to separate the metal 'tubes' supporting the LEDS so that more than 50 per cent of the screen was transparent. This significantly reduced the load to the supporting structure and in steel and ballast for the set.

Frederic Opsomer, founder and then head of System Technologies, developed the final idea which made the large-scale modular LED screen possible: frames for the LEDs that hinged together and would fold into place on a single dolly while maintaining alignment and protecting the electronics. This meant that a complete vertical strip of LEDS with their control electronics could be lifted into place, with connections only required at the top panel. The system could be rolled in and installed within three hours.

A typical large-scale show consists of a steel frame providing the supporting structure for the show elements – collectively termed 'the universal'. In the case of 'PopMart', this consisted of the largest LED screen ever built, at over 700 square metres (7,500 square feet); a 30-metre (98-foot) high golden arch of lightweight composite (the first large-scale use of this material in a touring stage); the PA system; a 3.8-metre (12-foot-6-inch) wide olive on a giant 30-metre (98-foot) cocktail stick; and a motorised 12-metre (39-foot) mirrorball lemon that would drive the band to the B-stage placed in the middle of the audience. The frequency with which touring shows must be performed to make them financially viable requires three steel sets leapfrogging

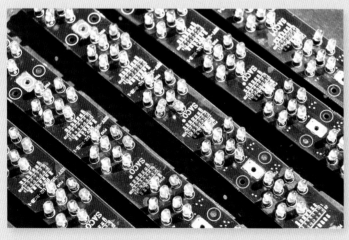

A strip of LED pixels, showing individual LEDs

The LED screen created for U2's 'PopMart' world tour (1997–8) consisted of 150,000 pixels, created by SACO Technologies, each containing eight separate LEDs of various colours, mounted in strips. The images are created by turning individual coloured LEDs within the pixels on or off, or adjusting their brightness. The closer together the pixels are, the higher the screen's resolution.

A strip of LED panels is being folded for transport. The pixels for the 'PopMart' tour's LED touring screen were mounted onto 4,500 separate aluminium tubes, which were arranged into 187 panels across 22 strips that folded for transport. The entire screen easily fitted into two trucks.

each other, so that as 'the universal' is loading out of one venue the next steel set is already being put in place at another.

Bridges and Ladders

One of the best things about working in the world of rock and roll is the absolute commitment to the work. Often in the building industry, if there is a problem the first reaction is to write a letter. If there is a problem in the rock-and-roll industry, the first reaction is to come together and fix it.

About six months before the Rolling Stones' 'Bridges to Babylon' tour (1997–8) was due to go out, STUFISH contacted Atelier One. The centrepiece for the stage set was to be a bridge which started the show beneath the stage. At the show's peak, the stage would open and the bridge would rise and extend out to meet a 6-metre (20-foot) square B-stage at the stadium's centre. The band would then shimmy over the bridge to perform a short 'intimate' set to 80,000 people.

The bridge was developed as a series of nesting U-shaped ladders which cantilevered out from the centre of the main stage and extended 43 metres (140 feet) across the audience, driven by a set of interlinking

STUFISH and Atelier One,
Arch structure for U2 'PopMart' world tour,
1997-8

The 100-metre (330-foot) parabolic golden arch, in the style of the McDonald's logo, was one of the 'PopMart' stage set's supersized illustrations of the tour's satirical theme of consumerism. It formed the centrepiece of the set design and also supported the PA system.

STUFISH and Atelier One,
The Rolling Stones 'Bridges
to Babylon' world tour,
1997-8

The 46-metre (150-foot) long cantilevered bridge's
telescoping structure can be seen here as it emerged
from underneath the main stage before extending to
the smaller B-stage in the centre of the audience about
50 metres (165 feet) away. Its design was inspired by
firemen's ladders, although on a grander scale.

STUFISH's designs for a tour are always
prototypes, because they are unique. Although
they are temporary structures, they undergo
full-scale testing, and must conform to stringent
building and fire safety codes to ensure the
stage sets are safe before being signed off to
tour internationally.

cables which would allow the U-sections to deploy together. With 19 weeks to go until the first show, Atelier One took the bridge to the West London Fire Brigade engine ladder builders, who said it would take two years to construct. Luckily, Brilliant Stages is one of the companies with which STUFISH has built a long-term collaborative relationship, and consists of people with the kind of skills which enabled them to put together the bridge's entire deployment system within the time limit.

However, the first full extension test at the workshop in West London did not go as it should have; just before completing full extension, a loud crack was heard and everything stopped. The 'Bridges to Babylon' tour had to get underway without a bridge until eight shows into the tour, when the bridge was air freighted to Atlanta, Georgia in the United States where it was successfully deployed and toured for another year and a half without incident.

Bridges and Arches

STUFISH's most ambitious entertainment design project to date was for the U2 '360°' world tour (2009–11). The title '360°' came from the set design, which allowed the audience to be placed in the round in large-scale stadium venues.

The design and its construction once again broke all previous rules for a stage set, being 100 per cent bespoke and completely groundbreaking. Nicknamed 'The Claw', the large four-legged structure was built above the stage, surmounted by the sound system and a cylindrical, expanding video screen. It was 50 metres

(164 feet) tall and the largest stage set ever constructed. Built by the specialist staging company Stageco in Belgium, its scale was such that it utilised bridge-building equipment to expedite installation – another first.

Because the structure was so light, it was ascertained that it could resonate at certain wind speeds. With the sophisticated analysis software then available, it was possible to predict the natural frequencies much more accurately than before. So, following the advice of Max Irvine, one of the world's eminent specialists in structural dynamics, it was decided active damping would be used and sloshing water dampers were chosen.

However, the staging company disagreed with Irvine's findings, arguing that damping would not be necessary. STUFISH responded to the effect that they could choose to take the dampers on tour as recommended and they would never know whether they had been necessary, or they could choose *not* to take them on tour and find out that they were. The dampers toured.

Organic Architecture

When STUFISH became heavily involved with large theatre developers in China, the opportunity presented itself to fulfil a long-held desire to get involved in creating more permanent architecture; it was apparent that sometimes no existing venues were available to adequately house the ambitious shows. In the case of the 75-minute acrobatic water spectacle created by show producers Dragone, it was agreed that STUFISH should design the theatre in which the show was to be housed. This had a quite obvious benefit in that

Atelier One for STUFISH design,
roof structure,
Dai Show Theatre,
Xishuangbanna,
Yunnan province, China,
2015

Responding to Xishuangbanna's warm climate and echoing its lush vegetation, the golden roof's layers act like a floating canopy of palm leaves over the 1,183-seat theatre's open-air lobby. At the junction of the two main tiers, openings allow visitors to look out onto the surrounding landscape and provide natural ventilation. Theatre space, architecture and landscape harmonise seamlessly.

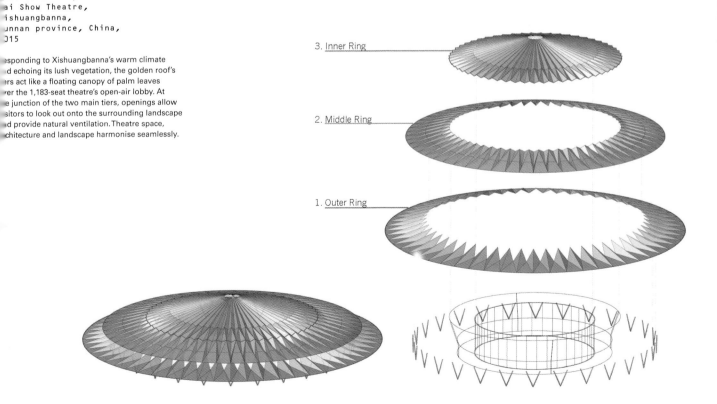

3. Inner Ring

2. Middle Ring

1. Outer Ring

the show's potential would no longer be constrained by the nature of an existing venue. The building for the Dai Show Theatre, Xishuangbanna, China (2015) was informed by nature, in particular the region's ubiquitous palm trees. This was expressed in the primary structure of the 110-metre (360-foot) diameter golden roof, with folds similar to the geometry of palm fronds that increase its structural rigidity. The building exterior uses folded plate rings in layers down the building, finally forming a huge continuous canopy ring around the perimeter which folds circumferentially and also hangs off the inner rings to create a structural skin that suggests 'look, no hands'. The same innovative qualities seen throughout STUFISH's work in touring shows were now successfully conveyed through permanent architecture.

Connections and Materials

Video screens in the early 1990s were basically large TV screens bolted together. They weighed 350 kilogrammes (750 pounds) per square metre and at 35 centimetres (14 inches) deep only two would fit on a standard touring cart at once. Move forward 25 years and LED screens now weigh 10 kilogrammes (22 pounds) per square metre and are 10 centimetres (4 inches) deep. With screens becoming ever larger, and with many using 600-plus individual panels, screens require precise and refined tolerances. The greatest conundrum for engineers was how to provide support for the screen and interface it with the steel framing. How best to transfer the load from the screen back to the ballast bases holding it stable?

Until U2's 'The Joshua Tree' world tours (2017 and 2019) this had involved an intricate web of secondary steelwork spanning between the primary frames and connected to each individual panel. To install this and make the many individual connections for every show was time-consuming and costly.

The solution came with the SpaceFrame system, developed by Frederic Opsomer, now of PRG Projects, with Atelier One and STUFISH. The idea was born to integrate the rigging and support structure with the panels themselves, allowing the panels to span between the primary frames without the intricate secondary steel structure. The proposed design was particularly clever in that the structure would lie flat for transport and unfold to its full depth only when in use. This meant that very thin transport dimensions could be maintained.

The greatest innovation, however, was the choice of material for the structure: carbon fibre – stronger than steel but only one fifth of the weight. SpaceFrame was hugely successful with the U2 production manager because it considerably reduces load-in and load-out times, the labour required on tour, and the set's weight and shipping footprint. The system, built of high-tech materials and designed to be lightweight, collapsible and fully wind braced, demonstrates a complete break with conventional wisdom and hints at an approach for the future of staging.

STUFISH, Atelier One and Frederic Opsomer/PRG Projects, U2 'The Joshua Tree' world tours, 2017 and 2019

Atelier One worked with PRG Projects on developing the support frame for what was then the largest, lightest LED screen ever developed. Rigging, support structure and wind bracing are integrated into the back of the ultra-light collapsible carbon-fibre SpaceFrame system. This allows artists and designers to adopt a more free-form approach to LED walls and stage designs.

SPACEFRAME IS A GOOD EXAMPLE OF HOW RECONSIDERING THE RECOGNISED APPROACH TO DESIGN CAN SUBVERT IT TO GOOD EFFECT

Touring Lightly

The issue of climate change now looms over everything we do, and discussions about the sustainability of touring and how this might be addressed have become a priority. For decades STUFISH, Atelier One and PRG have worked together to push the bounds of entertainment architecture and its possibilities. Their recently formed collaborative group, 'Major Tom', takes innovation further by re-imagining production processes, design and materials use in the events industry, with a focus on sustainability.

One of the main issues identified by the group is the need to plan touring more comprehensively, stockpiling elements of touring sets in locations of known major venues, negating the need for costly and carbon-intensive shipping around the world.

SpaceFrame is a good example of how reconsidering the recognised approach to design can subvert it to good effect. An important outcome of developing the SpaceFrame panel, for example, is the reduction of a tour's carbon footprint because less trucking is required.

Another ultra-light material, with similar qualities to carbon fibre and used for millennia, is bamboo. Millions of people around the world live in bamboo structures, and relatively recently advances in drying, treating and laminating bamboo have made it a commercially viable building material for more permanent structures. Bamboo is very special – it is strong, similar to steel in loadbearing capacity, light (one tenth the weight of steel) and extraordinarily sustainable. It grows phenomenally quickly: bamboo takes only four years to mature, sequestering tonnes of carbon during the process. To use bamboo for touring structures will require a shift in mindset and approach to design, but this kind of thinking is necessary to bring about reductions in carbon emissions. It is possible to envisage lightweight space frames of many forms, made of bamboo joined with bespoke connectors. Such structures would be capable of spanning large distances and supporting substantial loads, as is currently achieved using steel or aluminium, but at a fraction of the weight and with clear environmental benefits.

Bamboo is just one of many materials which, if utilised well, could create large, dramatic effects with limited resources. Membranes and nets are capable of spanning large distances with little material thanks to use of geometric (shape) stiffness. They can also fold into compact forms for easy transport. One could imagine combining these materials to create huge deployable screens in 3D forms, or filigree towers that can barely be perceived by audiences. The flexibility of the elements enables a myriad of possibilities to suit the individuality of the artists.

Anything is possible. A new language for concert touring is within achievable reach, with a cooperative approach from the industry worldwide. ⌂

Text © 2021 John Wiley & Sons Ltd. Images: pp 30–1 © Atelier One / Dick Bentley; p 35 © Atelier One; pp 36–7 © Atelier One / Chris Matthews; pp 32-4 © STUFISH

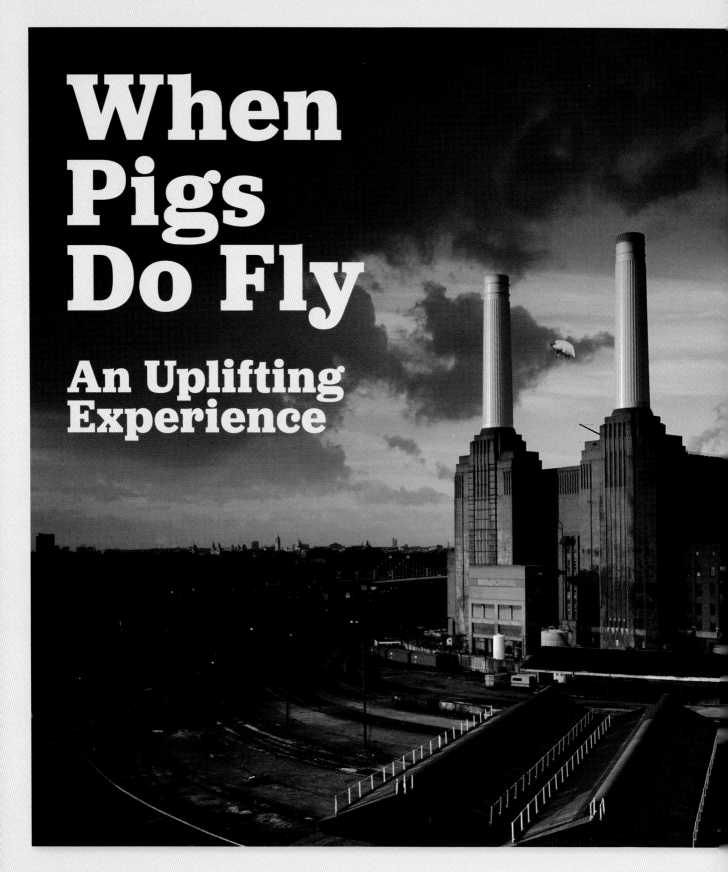

When Pigs Do Fly

An Uplifting Experience

Pink Floyd,
Animals album cover,
1977

The cover referenced the album's themes, which included George
Orwell's political, allegorical book *Animal Farm* (1945). The photograph,
by Aubrey Powell, shows a 12-metre (40-foot) pink inflatable pig floating
between two chimneys of the Battersea Power Station in London.
During the second day of photography, the balloon broke free of its
moorings and flew over Heathrow Airport, causing cancelled flights.

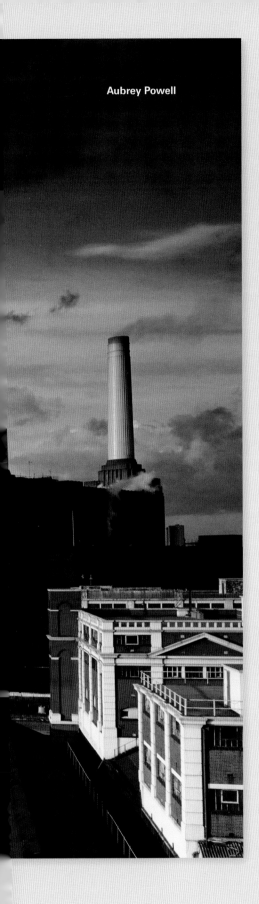

Aubrey Powell

Aubrey Powell started his creative life as the photographer and graphic designer for Hipgnosis, the acclaimed design studio he co-founded in 1967 with Storm Thorgerson. They were instrumental in defining Pink Floyd's graphic identity. Powell and Hipgnosis began working with Mark Fisher on the Pink Floyd 'Animals' world tour and album cover. It was a natural progression for Powell to move into filmmaking some 15 years later, when music video started. Here he describes some of his design collaborations with STUFISH.

I arrived at the first meeting at STUFISH carrying nothing more than a roll of lining paper and a black felt-tip pen. The discussion was to be about working together on the 'Pink Floyd: Their Mortal Remains' exhibition at London's Victoria and Albert Museum (V&A), and although highly experienced as a creative director, I was a novice when it came to filling 17,000 square feet (1,600 square metres) of Victorian architecture. One could have heard a pin drop as I began to draw the basic ideas, unrolling the paper as they began to take form. Once the sketch had been completed, the STUFISH team embraced many of the initial thoughts with confidence and three years later the project bore fruit. 'Pink Floyd: Their Mortal Remains' opened to great acclaim in May 2017 and was to be the best-attended and most successful exhibition the V&A had ever produced.

Successful entertainment architecture is very much about synergy: between the entertainers and the audience; between the entertainers and the architecture; and between the entertainers and the architects who are constructing something designed to be looked at by an audience, and that allows the audience to be stimulated and inspired by what they see. It does not matter if it is a rock-and-roll set, a theatre set, a film set or an exhibition. Moreover, the environment in which entertainment architecture is created is uniquely multifaceted and complex, teeming with logistical nightmares, professionals whose needs must be accommodated, and fastidiously creative individuals with brittle egos and the insecurities that can come with constant exposure to the public's adoring – or critical – gaze.

An exhibition, although static, is a complex form of entertainment architecture. It is a cultural exchange, not just a series of display cases one looks into. It has themes of concept, form, materials, connection and construction. For the V&A exhibition, Pink Floyd wanted something with gravitas, something that was larger than life, something which really interpreted the Pink Floyd experience. And Pink Floyd is probably one of the biggest and most innovative bands in the world. So one could not shrink away from that, or be boring or predictable.

As creative director for the exhibition, my decision to approach STUFISH as the team's architects had been made after careful consideration. One obvious reason, aside from having worked with them in the past, was because STUFISH already had a long history with the band. That meant their imagination was capable of working within the Pink Floyd framework. They were also the only people with the crossover understanding of really inventive architectural design, theatrical experience and the rock-and-roll genre. Their reputation, and seeing what they had done for Pink Floyd, Lady Gaga and U2, made it clear they would not be constricted by traditional ideas of glass boxes with display units.

The concept I had in mind at that initial meeting was chronological, running through all the Pink Floyd albums in order. Like the band's career, it began simply:

STUFISH,
Internal elevation for 'Pink Floyd:
Their Mortal Remains' exhibition,
Victoria and Albert Museum, London,
May–October 2017

This CAD drawing is an unwrapped elevation of the wall in the V&A's exhibition. The wall was simplified and changed in future iterations. In Pink Floyd's original tour of their *The Wall* album, in an unusual application of architectural principles to musical staging, the wall was built brick by brick, eventually separating the audience from the performers' act.

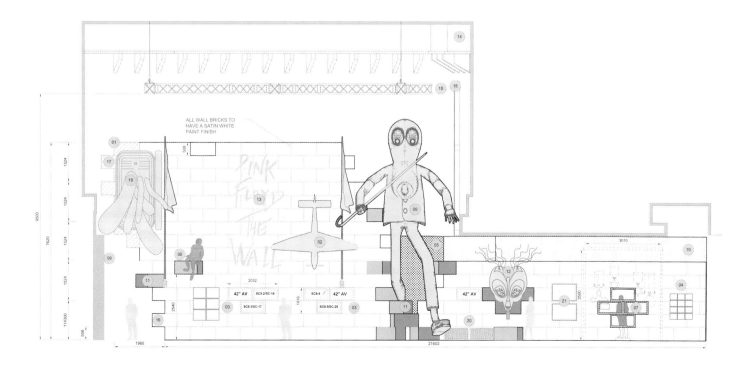

STUFISH and Aubrey Powell,
Pink Floyd: Their Mortal Remains' exhibition,
Victoria and Albert Museum, London,
May-October 2017

The exhibition entrance was a walk-through, oversized replica
of Pink Floyd's beaten-up old Bedford van, used to take them
from gig to gig during the band's early years in the mid-1960s.
They customised the van with a single, diagonal white line
which made it instantly recognisable wherever they went.

Attention to detail was essential, because the participants would study the artefacts and because, as a museum, the V&A prides itself on its accuracy of information and learning

the exhibition entrance was through a replica of the band's famous Bedford van, and continued through a psychedelic corridor to display cases containing various fun artefacts relating to Pink Floyd during the late 1960s and early 1970s. It was still what might be considered an ordinary museum environment. Then, the visitor would arrive at the display marking the album *The Dark Side of the Moon*, when the world exploded for Pink Floyd in March 1973. They became the biggest band in the world and sold 65 million albums. At that point, the traditional showcases were left behind and another world began: a holographic world with an amazing immersive sound system from Sennheiser 360 degrees audio headsets, and suddenly visitors would be enveloped in a magical fantasy land.

Attention to detail was essential, because the participants would study the artefacts and because, as a museum, the V&A prides itself on its accuracy of information and learning. STUFISH also had to adapt and create a show that could be put up and taken down and travel safely to any venue, globally. It was enormously challenging.

Collaboration and the Creative Process

STUFISH's lack of arrogance and willingness to play back and forth to achieve the right design structure played a large part in how quickly the process went from discussions with Ray Winkler, sketching out, building the maquette, and on to the plans and elevations. Collaborative effort is an important point in all our creative lives. There is never a singularity that defines what an exhibition or a show must become. Effective collaboration requires a non-territorial

A key point in the collaborative process came after a few months, when the drawings and elevations showed the team was going in the right direction. It was very colourful and very bright

attitude and way of thinking in which respect and trust exist, so that each person's contribution is not an end in itself but part of a common endeavour to create something extraordinary.

What was interesting was that Ray and the others seemed to grasp the ideas immediately and run with them. They understood what was being talked about; even though some of the team did not know much about Pink Floyd, they understood the big picture. There was to be the inflatable pig (of which more later); we had to have the Wall from the album of that name; we had to have the two huge statues from the cover of the album *The Division Bell*; there had to be showcases that illustrated the early parts of their career. Having been handed the ingredients, it was obvious STUFISH were going to come up with something interesting.

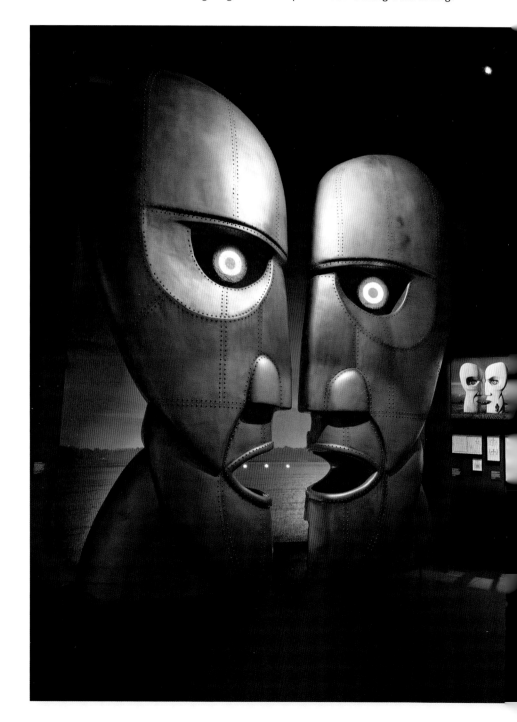

Hipgnosis and Keith Breeden,
Sculptures for Pink Floyd's
The Division Bell album (1994),
'Pink Floyd: Their Mortal
Remains' exhibition,
Victoria and Albert Museum,
London,
May-October 2017

For the cover of the album *The Division Bell*, two 4.5-metre (15-foot) metal heads designed by Hipgnosis's Storm Thorgerson and the artist Keith Breeden were photographed positioned in a field near Cambridge, England. The single eyes of the faces regarding each other become the eyes of a ghostly single face looking at the viewer.

A key point in the collaborative process came after a few months, when the drawings and elevations showed the team was going in the right direction. It was very colourful and very bright. And the sets were huge – the Wall was enormous, and of great tumbling bricks with the Teacher character from the *Wall* album peering over the top, exactly as envisioned. But the pivotal moment came one day when I tried on the Oculus virtual-reality headset at STUFISH. Suddenly, the three-dimensional world whose design had been conceived in two dimensions came to life. The sudden realisation that the exhibition was coming together in the way it had been envisaged and that I could walk through and see exactly what it would be like, was a moment of revelation. It was uncannily, almost miraculously, accurate. STUFISH had got it; they were there, and they were already moving towards a future where it is possible to work in an unreal world that actually denotes a real world.

While the Pink Floyd project was still underway, I was asked by the surreal comedy collective Monty Python to direct a film of their ten-night show *Monty Python Live (Mostly): One Down, Five to Go* at the O2 stadium in London. It was a great relief to know STUFISH were designing the stage. It meant working with people who combined scope and breadth of experience as entertainment designers with a fundamental understanding of camera placement, lighting and sound for television, film and stage work.

The collaborative process for this live event was very different from that of the V&A exhibition. This was a complex show, of quick-changeover sets, quick-change costume issues, musical song-and-dance numbers, ageing performers who had not worked together for years, and an untried orchestra.

It was also a complex shoot. As the film director, I had to negotiate with set designers, lighting designers, wardrobe people, hair and makeup people, an army of technicians, recording people, video assistants, screen directors, choreographers, stage directors, camera operators. It was STUFISH's responsibility to design a stage set that would make the show itself seamless. Transitions between comedy vignettes and musical interludes had to flow in terms of costume and musical changes and artists' entrances and exits. The design also had to satisfy a nightly audience of 17,000 people, while accommodating lighting and sound rigs and 20 television cameras that needed unobstructed visual access to the stage.

Just as with the V&A exhibition, attention to detail was crucial, although in this case it was more like making sure all the gears and cogwheels in a Swiss watch meshed perfectly. STUFISH had to adjust, fine-tune, and work fast and patiently to adhere to the artists' requirements. It could get very tense. STUFISH, with Ric Lipson at the helm, was central and pivotal to the process of creating the conditions which allowed open discussion and collaboration to take place, whether it involved access to the nearest toilet for the artist or flying a huge and dangerous lighting and sound rig over the proscenium without obstructing the TV cameras.

That is what real entertainment architects do; they are capable of working in any environment, with any kind of entertainment. They have the ability to be constantly creative and adaptable, enabling the entire team's creativity without arrogance or rigidity. It is a real skill, and rare in the industry.

Narrative, Memory and Magic

Although the architecture of exhibitions and live shows differs greatly, a unifying element bridging the two genres is the manipulation of three-dimensional space to create narrative and atmosphere – which all architecture does in a sense, though perhaps not as deliberately or on the same scale as entertainment architecture. The emotional potency of these narratives can pass through into the real world and remain long after an entertainment event is history, as happened during the process of turning London's Battersea Power Station into a two-dimensional album cover, and then back into a three-dimensional set piece for the Pink Floyd exhibition years later.

In 1977 Roger Waters, Pink Floyd's co-founder, decided that the band needed to create more theatrical events around their concerts, so he developed the idea of dirigibles for the 'Animals' world tour. The first idea he came up with was a pig, which was actually designed by the Australian artist Jeffrey Shaw. Waters and I had a meeting and decided to fly the pig over the monumental, iconic late Art Deco Battersea Power Station. The *Animals* album is very Orwellian; dogs, pigs and sheep are included in the storyline. It also is about 'us and them' – about the 'haves' and the 'have nots'. And the dereliction of Battersea Power Station was shocking at that time. This, arguably the grandest red-brick edifice in the whole of Europe was falling apart and surrounded by rubble and detritus. Roger felt it represented the lyrics he had written. So he got the pig, and we arranged the time, and flew the pig out of the power station to photograph it for the album cover.

That is what real entertainment architects do; they are capable of working in any environment, with any kind of entertainment

STUFISH,
'Monty Python Live (Mostly):
One Down Five to Go' show,
O2 Arena, London,
July 2014

right: This concept render shows the stage layout with multiple entrances and positions for scenic trucks – moving platforms on which scenery is built to facilitate scene changes. There were 40 different scenes created during the show for the various sketches – some that used only one entrance each, and some that used all three.

below: Created to fill the width of the O2 Arena, the stage was stylised to look like a pop-up toy theatre with painted graphics from iconic Terry Gilliam illustrations. Designed to enable both large-scale scenes with the full cast of Pythons and dancers, and intimate sketches created for close-up cameras and relayed on the side screens, it also had to work simultaneously for the live arena audience and for the filmed version streamed live worldwide and captured for DVD.

EXPLANATION OF ENTRANCES AND SCENERY TRUCKS

MONTY PYTHON LIVE (mostly) | ILLUSTRATIONS | 13 JANUARY 2014 |

44

By now everyone knows it escaped and made headlines around the world. The incident drew attention to Pink Floyd and what they were about, but also to the Battersea Power Station and its architect, Giles Gilbert Scott, and to the fact that Scott designed England's iconic red telephone box. It was a major PR coup for Pink Floyd, and as a result Battersea itself became a focal point for preservation and restoration. Then, during the opening film for the 2012 London Olympics opening ceremony, during the bird's-eye view of the Thames coming up to the Battersea Power Station, there was a pink pig floating in the air, and suddenly there was the realisation that this graphic image – conceived for an album cover – has become a potent symbol for London and the association with Battersea Power Station.

STUFISH and Aubrey Powell,
 Pink Floyd: Their Mortal Remains' exhibition,
Victoria and Albert Museum, London,
May–October 2017

The 'Architecture' section of the exhibition, showing STUFISH founder Mark Fisher's work in the context of objects from the V&A architectural collections, was nestled within the 9-metre (30-foot) high parallax view stage set of the Battersea Power Station, which dissolved into separate sections on closer inspection. The London landmark, designed by J. Theo Halliday and Giles Gilbert Scott and completed in 1941, was pictured on the cover of Pink Floyd's *Animals* album.

To see it take form again in the exhibition 'Pink Floyd: Their Mortal Remains' as a replica was a nice full circle. Originally it had been envisaged as a model, but that would have lost the building's huge scale. STUFISH decided instead to build a large replica of the power station as a piece of scenic art with a parallax effect. So the towering scale was retained, with the pig flying above it. It was visual trickery – magic – of a very clever kind. And this magic is the essence of where the power of entertainment architecture lies. Patrick Woodroffe's amazing lighting for the exhibition enhanced this, as did the shiny black flooring STUFISH installed, which reflected light and the surrounding environment into the floor. It felt as if you were walking on water – and it was a transcendent experience.

This was true entertainment architecture, which is about creating worlds that do not really exist. People want to be transported – they do not want to think about the bother of COVID, they do not want the bother of Brexit, they do not want the bother of financial issues, they want to be taken out of all that. And if you can succeed in creating a space where people move into a magic land – a fantasy world, but a fantasy world with sophistication – then you have succeeded on every level. ⌂

LIG
REVEALING T

Patrick Woodroffe

H T

E UNSEEN

STUFISH and Woodroffe Bassett
Design (WBD) (lighting),
The Rolling Stones
'No Filter' tour,
Hamburg,
2017

The stage architecture had the look of
stripped-back industrial chic and modern
simplicity. A catwalk and B-stage took the
action into the audience, while the stage
itself was dominated by four monolithic,
22-metre (72-foot) tall, 11-metre (36-foot)
wide LED screen towers. LED returns at the
sides of each tower created a unique 3D
appearance, while recessed lights at the top
and sides offered a magnificent light show
while enhancing the minimalist look.

With four decades of diverse experience illuminating numerous performative events, **Patrick Woodroffe**, a senior partner of international lighting consultancy Woodroffe Bassett Design, explains the importance of light to performer and scenery. He also gives us an insight into some of his interactions with various performers and then runs us through the sorts of things a typical day entails.

Light in its abstract form is an arbitrary concept. Its extraordinary power is felt in a thousand ways in our daily lives, yet even as we aware of its effect, we never actually *see* it. Except perhaps in the work of theatrical lighting designers.

Passing through the filter of a manufactured haze of smoke, the light we work with takes on a dimension and a plasticity that can be moulded and coloured, giving shape to the air around it. The light can be focused as sharp as a laser beam or flooded out to cover huge areas of space. It can be physically moved about the stage in patterns and shapes. It can be made to appear or disappear in an instant. It can slowly conjure a piece of architecture out of thin air and then fade away as quietly and as modestly as it arrived. And in its complet absence, the darkness that remains is as acutely real and powerful as the light it has replaced.

STUFISH and Woodroffe Bassett Design (WBD) (lighting),
Steve Wynn's Showstoppers,
Encore Theater, Wynn Hotel,
Las Vegas,
2014

The image shows a scene from the musical *Showstoppers.* The production for the show was old-style in its technique and execution, inspired by the legendary Broadway musicals of the past. There were no video screens, and the visual aesthetic was glamorous, soft and sensual, using velvet and glitter fabrics that reflected the light beautifully to create an aura of opulence.

Stepping the Light Fantastic

The medium means nothing, of course, without a subject to light, just as the scenery on a stage has no real purpose or form until it is illuminated. Once lit, though, it is the transformative nature of light that is both an effect in itself as well being the torch that reveals the hidden architecture that was there all along.

Mark Fisher and I understood this very early on in our collaboration as we explored the idea that lighting and scenery were indivisible. Not in some philosophical manner, but really quite literally. We wanted to break the traditional approach – that of an architectural form set firmly on the ground with a lighting rig hanging above it – and instead went about consciously integrating the two.

One of the first and most important examples of this approach was the ground-breaking production that was the Rolling Stones' 'Steel Wheels' tour in 1989. Mark's derelict, dystopian factory of the future had at its heart six giant rectangular lights, each the size of a small car, which surrounded the stage platform. These fixtures were fitted with giant scrolls of coloured gel that rolled across the face of the lights, creating great swathes of deep, saturated colour that changed the form of the stage completely. The lights themselves were the scenery, and every other scenic element – the over-scaled industrial trusses, rows of metallic balustrades and giant curving staircase – all these structures had the rest of the lighting system actually built into them.

From then on, in every project that our two practices undertook and in the collaborations that continued with the STUFISH studio, the boundary between scenic design and lighting became less defined. One discipline guided the other with no apparent rule, and it was this seamless amalgamation of both disciplines that resulted in a hybrid form of design where it was difficult to tell where one began and the other ended.

After the scenery and the lighting, the third partner in any design project is the performer. The job of the creative team is to provide a setting in which the character of the artist is somehow manifest in the design, but where the aim is also to interpret the narrative of their performance. In theatre or opera the script notes can be practical and even mundane 'Sunlight streamed through the French windows!' or 'The curtain lifts on a colourful ball thrown by the Capulet family!'. And we light accordingly.

But the interpretation of live music is a much more subjective and visceral exercise. I always make the effort to explain to the artists with whom I work exactly what it is that I am doing and why I am making the choices that I do, and consequently, on many occasions the result is that we make those choices together. Understandably, this approach did not work with Stevie Wonder with whom I toured for the first time in 1985. Although I could explain to him the idea that a certain colour might express a particular emotion, the concept of sight, of a missing sense, was elusive. But then it struck me that although I could not explain what vision was – Stevie used to call it 'that other thing' – I had the ability

Fisher Park Partnership and Patrick Woodroffe (lighting), The Rolling Stones 'Steel Wheels' tour, North America and Japan, 1989-90

The big-budget stadium rock-concert tour included a light show, exploding fireworks and towers that shot out flames on the massive stage. It was ground-breaking in its use of six giant lights to, in essence, continuously create and re-create the scenery during the show, while the structure and lighting were unified in the other scenic elements.

STUFISH and Woodroffe Bassett
Design (WBD) (lighting),
Elton John 'Farewell Yellow
Brick Road' world tour,
Allentown, Pennsylvania,
2018

The massive LED screen, which flows onto the stage,
is surrounded by a sculpted gold frame that wraps
around the front of the stage in a great Baroque
curve, illustrating aspects of Elton John's life. Lights
and gilding, reflecting his love of opulence, weave
throughout the sinuous structure. WBD worked with
lighting and video programmers to integrate the two
elements to give each song its own distinctive look.

to deliberately take that same sense away from the
audience. And more to the point, as it would be Stevie
who would signal the moment himself, they would
understand that the gesture was a conscious invitation
for us to enter his world. It was his gift.

Every night, midway through the set, he would lean
into his mic and say quietly, 'Hey, Patrick, can you turn
out all the lights?' As he began to play the opening
chords of 'Visions of My Mind', we would slowly fade
the stage to complete darkness. The musicians would
turn off their music-stand lights, the technicians would
dim their control boards, and for the next seven and a
half minutes we were all inside Stevie Wonder's head.
Performer and audience were united as never before.

Keeping the Artist in the Dark
In general, most artists want to be part of the lighting
process and understandably so. After all, each of their
songs is their own creation, a piece of music that has
been conceived with a particular meaning and emotion
in mind. How the lighting designer interprets that
feeling in terms of colour and mood is a subjective
choice and so hugely important to the artist. But this
is not always the case. In 2011, six months before the
premiere of his new show at Caesars Palace in Las
Vegas, Elton John asked that we tell him absolutely
nothing about the design of his show at all. He insisted
he did not want to see any models, drawings or sketches
until the moment he walked on to the stage for his dress
rehearsal, allowing him the visceral thrill of getting the
whole thing in one hit – just as his audience would the
next night. It was an extraordinary gesture of faith.

Keith Richards was less interested in the way the set actually looked than he was in the way that it felt. He often referred to the stage as his office, once telling me: 'I love what you are doing upstairs, but I really only need to see where I'm going on the ground floor!' Generally, though, artists want to be involved in the minutiae, and although challenging at times as opinions differ, when the team is united there is no better feeling. After all, who would not want Bob Dylan to nod approvingly at one's work? Even if it were an enigmatic nod, and one unaccompanied by mere words.

From the mid-1970s onwards, the rock-and-roll touring industry very much led the way in the development of the technology it used. As the demand from audiences grew, so did the scale of the venues in which the shows took place – from theatres to sports arenas and finally to stadia that held up to 100,000 people. Sound systems had to be larger and more powerful to fill these larger venues; video screens were required to show the artists in close-up, and the lighting had to be that much more spectacular.

STUFISH and Patrick Woodroffe (lighting), Elton John 'The Million Dollar Piano' concert residency, The Colosseum at Caesars Palace, Las Vegas, Nevada, 2011-18

STUFISH's concept was to present Elton John as the 'Sun King' of Las Vegas, referencing architecture and sculpture from the height of the European Baroque. The scenery combined hand-carved and gilded sculpture with 21st-century computerised lighting technology. The custom-built million-dollar Yamaha piano incorporated 68 LED video screens that could display imagery synchronising with the imagery on stage or interpreting the emotions expressed in the music the artist was playing.

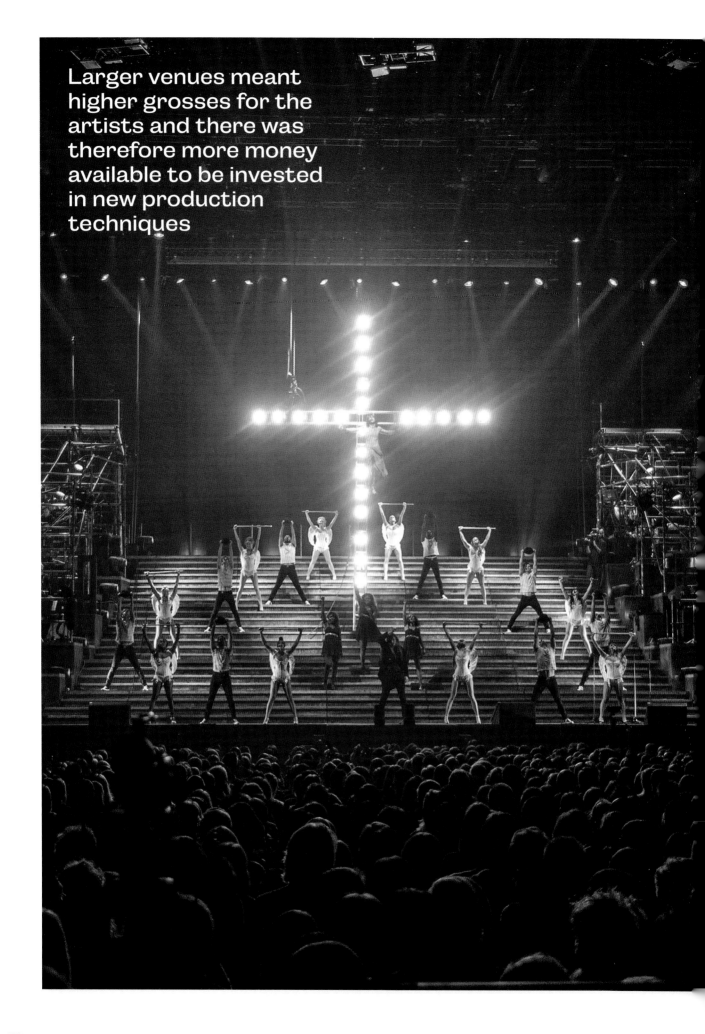

Larger venues meant higher grosses for the artists and there was therefore more money available to be invested in new production techniques

These larger venues meant higher grosses for the
artists and there was therefore more money available
to be invested in new production techniques. The first
automated light that could move position, and change
colour and intensity remotely, was called the Varilite,
which was developed in 1984. From that moment
on, everything changed. It was as if we had a new
superpower. These extraordinary lighting systems
became the tools with which we were able to create
animated light paintings. This was life drawing on
a grand scale, and although the process of creating
a whole show could take days or even weeks to
complete, the actual process, the throwing down
of light and colour onto the canvas of a stage, was
instantaneous and therefore incredibly satisfying.

A music tour has a lot of practical requirements
that have to be taken into account at the same time as
the art is being considered. The first part of a project
steers a lot of the decisions as to the amount of lights,
where they are sourced, how they are rigged and how
they fit it into the general nature of the design. And of
course there is the budget to consider. But it is when
this part of the process is completed and the team
gathers together for the first time in a rehearsal studio
that the magic begins. The Cirque du Soleil director
Franco Dragone talked about this process of turning the
various visual and sonic elements of a production into
a show as 'Creation'. For us, Creation is the journey of
discovery through light.

STUFISH and Patrick Woodroffe (lighting),
Genesis 'Turn It On Again' tour,
Munich,
2007

This 75-metre (250-foot) wide curved screen, composed of
more than 15,000 separate LED display tiles, could be erected
in under three hours. It hung from a curved fascia truss
that itself contained an array of intelligent lights and all the
rigging for the screen. Woodroffe and STUFISH collaborated
very closely to amalgamate the live show, lighting and video
effects in a seamless fusion of visual elements.

A Timeline of Creation

4.00 am: There are less than a dozen of us in the empty arena – three lighting programmers and myself, a few technicians, and a bored security guard who looks at his watch as he tips back in his chair.

Sitting in the middle of the enormous space like an island is our control position. Angle-poise lamps with amber gels cast a comfortable glow over the lighting desks, and the cheap carpet on the riser creates a semblance of comfort. The floor around us is empty except for a few scattered road boxes and a thick umbilical cord of cables. On the floor lies the detritus of rehearsal – empty coffee cups, plates of half-eaten food, pieces of paper with scratched notes on them. The only sounds are the clack, clack, clack of the computer keys, an occasional crackle of a walkie-talkie, and the distant roar of the generators that produce the power to run the huge lighting system.

At the other end of the arena is the enormous stage, stretching from one side of the building to the other and reaching high up into the rafters. It is a marvel of engineering, enormously expensive and full of lights and effects, but now it simply mocks us, holding so much promise that we have yet to discover.

It's late and I'm cold, tired and hungry. Eight songs into the show and I know it's not right. The focus is messy and the smoke haze that we use to register the lighting beams is weak. There is no dynamic in the work. Everything is starting to look the same, with no character or personality to the lighting states. The colours are weak, but when we saturate them the stage looks too dark.

STUFISH and Woodroffe Bassett
Design (WBD) (lighting),
Lady Gaga 'Born This Way Ball'
world tour,
2012–13

One of the most complex pieces of set design
ever created, the three-storey castle, with
LED lighting integrated into the structure's
architectural details, was set with turrets and
staircases that acted as performance spaces.
Its kinetic doors could open and close to
reveal windows, doors, moving staircases
and rooms. An overhead track allowed a
floating holographic face of 'Mother G.O.A.T'
– a rotating, transparent prism that contained
an animatronic replica of Lady Gaga's face
with prosthetics – to move through the sky
above the stage.

*One of the programmers is involved in building
a complicated chase sequence and is concentrated
at his control board, head bent, fingers flying over
the keyboards as they beat out an incessant cha-cha-
cha, his lips silently calling out numbers to himself,
trying to keep track of what he's doing, trying to turn
science into art. Lights swing out across the room in
meaningless rhythm, lighting up the dreary hanger.
I'm falling asleep now. My head drops, strange
half-awake dreams run through my brain, echoes,
ideas – I jerk awake again, get up and try to find
some energy.*

*Then someone kills the ugly work-light in the
back corner of the room. The smoke thickens; we run
the new sequence – yes that looks better. We take
out some more lights and use the darkness. Less
is better now, let's save more till later. We run the
number again, thin out the cues, move the chase
back to the end of the song, double the brightness on
the last chorus, then run it one more time. Everyone
excited now. I turn up the music, banging out the
beat on the table, snapping the cues with my fingers.*

The security guard smiles.

It is never a straightforward journey and the
challenge of bringing together all the pieces of a
production is not to be underestimated. But when
it does all come together on the opening night, the
pay-off is enormous. Architecture and light; emotion
and music; artist and audience; smoke and mirrors.
All connected to make a whole that is so much
greater than the sum of its parts. ⌂

Lonely Together

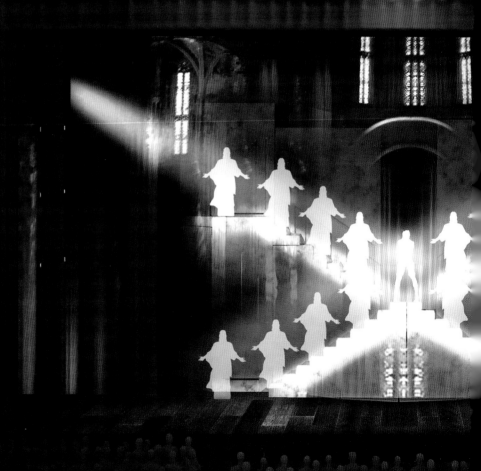

STUFISH,
Madonna 'Madame X' tour,
August 2019

Concept illustration of Madonna's
'Like a Prayer' showing the
multilayered set design and intimate
environment between the stage and
audience. Disguise video-mapping
technology was used to project over
the STUFISH-designed kinetic 3D
set, stage background and theatre
architecture, immersing the audience
and performers in the scene.

Ash Nehru

The Coming Confluence of Virtual and Real

Ash Nehru is a co-founder of Disguise — a platform that allows creative ideas to combine with software and media server hardware technologies of the sort regularly employed by STUFISH's productions to bring digital video layers into their physical staging designs. Here he examines the use of mixed realities for contemporary performance and their continued potential as new technologies come online.

I remember my first 'gig' as a 'punter' like it was yesterday. For an introverted computer geek, it was life-changing – the clamour and the thunder, the pulse and swirl of the mosh pit, the elbow in the face; the shouted communion, the joyous transcendence. Not bad for an Edie Brickell concert.

Shed a tear, then, for the sequestered children of the Internet age, who have never tasted (and may never taste) the rough joys of the live show; whose formative concert-going experience was Travis Scott playing 'live' (27 April 2020) in the video game *Fortnite*: just a blizzard of polygons on a screen in their bedroom. They haven't truly *lived*, these kids today, runs the refrain; let us pity them.

Like it or not, however, the virtual genie is out of the bottle. As virtual reality continues its inexorable progress towards maturity (backed by the might of Facebook and Apple), virtual experiences will become ever-more immersive, compelling and accessible – ever more *normal*. If nothing else, the audience numbers (20 million for the Travis Scott show) mean that the live industry cannot afford to ignore this new medium.

Nor should it. We romanticise the live experience, but the truth is, away from the privileged 'front of house' zone that the designer inhabits, the 'mega-concert' experience can be a snore. From up at the back of the stadium, or off to the side, all that spectacle is nothing more than a doll's house, that much-vaunted 'communion' just a sea of mobile phones pointed at a big television. Ironically, as someone who has made a career of building tools for designers to visualise and create such experiences, I am happiest in tiny clubs, up close to musicians jamming, with no need for the Death Star technology I peddle.

But it is not a zero-sum game. Film did not herald the obsolescence of theatre, nor filmed concerts the end of live shows. What we are seeing today is an explosion of experimentation in the creation of virtual worlds, and new ways of blending them with the real. Instead of a fight to the death, why not work for a cross-fertilisation between the 'old' and 'new' art-forms that enriches both?

Nurse, The Screens

Stage designers are servants to two competing imperatives: they have to create spectacle, but also deliver the intimacy that the audience truly craves. Once your fanbase grows above a certain size, it is no longer commercially sustainable to play small shows. Madonna's 'Madame X' tour (2019–20) was a typically fearless attempt to return to the intimacy of her early years – theatre audiences of just 2,500 people, mobile phones forbidden, and high ticket prices. But as a consequence, to reach just a small fraction of her global audience, she had to play 75 shows – not a particularly sustainable approach.

A desire to bring *all* fans to the live experience leads inexorably to larger venues as a performer grows in stature; first arenas, then stadiums, then Knebworth.

But that scale means that for most of the audience, the performer is just a distant speck of starlight. If the audience cannot see the star, you have to give them *something* to look at. That *something* had better be as dazzling as all that ticket revenue can buy, and definitely has to out-dazzle the competition. That simple commercial equation led to an arms-race of spectacle that drove, and benefited from, advances in stage technology.

In prehistoric times (sometimes referred to as 'the seventies'), show designers were restricted to using lights. They had to light the performers, but also create a dazzling light *show*, turning the lighting rig into a musical instrument in itself. The advent of high-brightness projection, and later LED screens, finally gave designers a way to deliver a simulacrum of intimacy to large audiences. IMAG (image magnification) uses close-up live camera views of the performers, presented on large screens placed above or outside the 'pure' stage design.

Screens, of course, can be used for more than just live images – they can deliver art, graphics, animation, abstraction, messages and more. The most adroit performers engaged with this capability and delivered shows that entered the culture: for example U2's 'PopMart' (1997–8) or Pink Floyd's 'The Wall' (1980–1). This created a further challenge for designers: balancing the needs of IMAG and 'art' content so that they form a harmonious whole rather than competing with each other.

As technology has progressed, we have escaped the constricting rectangular frame and reimagined screens as sculptural surfaces, such as the Robbie Williams 3D video face in 2013. The rise of media servers (powerful computers that can visualise and play video on complex or moving shapes) give the designer an ever-expanding palette of techniques to build 'video environments' that surround and interact with the performance.

The Rise of Real Time

Traditional video content has to be generated (or 'rendered') before the concert, which is expensive and slow, and not unstressful when deadlines loom. Real-time content, by contrast, is rendered 'on the fly' during the show, like a video game. This means it can be changed relatively quickly (handy when pop stars change their minds, as they occasionally do), and can respond to live camera feeds, audio and MIDI (Musical Instrument Digital Interface). This makes it 'live' in a way that traditional video can never be; effectively, it is a graphical 'instrument' to add to the band.

Early real-time content was 'hacked together' by the handful of show-makers who could write code, which restricted its accessibility. In the 2010s, however, the advent of commercial tools (such as TouchDesigner and Notch) put this power into the hands of artists and led to an explosion in the use of real-time graphics in live concerts. More recently, commercial games engines such as Unity and Unreal, backed by millions

STUFISH,
Robbie Williams
'Take the Crown' tour,
Brussels,
May 2013

A large, oval, custom-LED screen
was created as the backdrop for this
performance. Designed by STUFISH,
in the centre was the world's first,
tourable, 3D LED-screen sculpture
that took its form from a 3D scan of
Williams's face. The complex piece was
sculpted in foam and moulded in fibre
glass before each pixel was individually
added to make the screen surface.
Disguise wrote custom video-mapping
code to play back the video content
onto the video-screen surfaces.

TUFISH,
ueen + Adam Lambert
Rhapsody' world tour,
acoma, Washington,
uly 2019

e first act of this ongoing spectacular rock
ow reveals the band inside a bespoke styled
era house shown on the LED screens. In
s STUFISH stage design, with video content
eated by Treatment Studio inside Notch
ftware and played back though the Disguise
edia server, the opera house architecture and
apes are fully live rendered 3D objects that
spond to the stage lighting and shadows to
pear real.

Cluster rendering: set-up and components

Add multiple rx nodes to scale out your rendering depending on the size of your production .

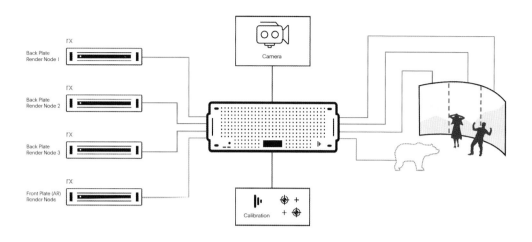

Disguise,
Cluster-rendering setup for
the Disguise media server,
2020

This setup allows multiple render node computers to scale out the rendering to adapt to the size of the production. This means that video-screen elements can be higher resolution, and with content created to immerse performers on the fly.

of dollars and thousands of engineers, have further expanded its potential. Early uses trended towards live processing the IMAG feed, and simple abstract effects such as lighting, particle fields and graphics. As technology advanced, however, it became possible to simulate ever-more complex and realistic three-dimensional worlds. The latest Queen tour, for instance, creates a virtually-lit opera house as a live environment for the band.

Until now, however, the quality and complexity of real-time graphics have been limited by the power of the graphics processors that do the rendering, leading some artists to reject it for its 'video-game' aesthetic. This is about to change: an innovation called 'clustered rendering', which marshals large groups of machines to collaborate on the rendering, enables the creation of virtual scenes every bit as realistic as those in films, in real time, at massive scale. And this, in turn, sets the scene for the next chapter of show design: extended reality.

Reality, Extended

For decades, computer interaction researchers have fantasised about augmented reality, or AR – the idea that we will one day interact with computers by wearing fancy sunglasses that can make 'holographic' objects appear in front of us. Undaunted by decades of failure to create actual AR glasses, the industry has instead delivered a cut-down version of AR that runs on mobile phones. Most commonly experienced as 'fun filters' in apps like Snapchat and Instagram, AR has become a normal part of the social media experience for millions of people. It was therefore only a matter of time before show designers wanted to get in on the action.

Since most live concerts are already a sea of mobile phones, this seemed like a natural fit, and it has been used by some of the more forward-thinking performers, including U2 on their 'eXPERIENCE + iNNOCENCE' world tour (2018). The drawback is that you have to download

STUFISH, Willie Williams and Es Devlin Studio,
U2 'eXPERIENCE + iNNOCENCE' world tour,
Tulsa, Oklahoma,
May 2018

Mr MacPhisto was originally a character in the 1992 'Zoo TV' show where Bono would paint his face with makeup. This resurrection in 2018 applies a digital makeup. STUFISH worked with Facebook and the Reality Augmented Studio company to create a bespoke digital filter that allowed Bono to transform himself, live. A camera was incorporated into a mirror that he could look into and be augmented. The signal was then projected onto the large screen. An example of AR technology being used in a live show as a storytelling device.

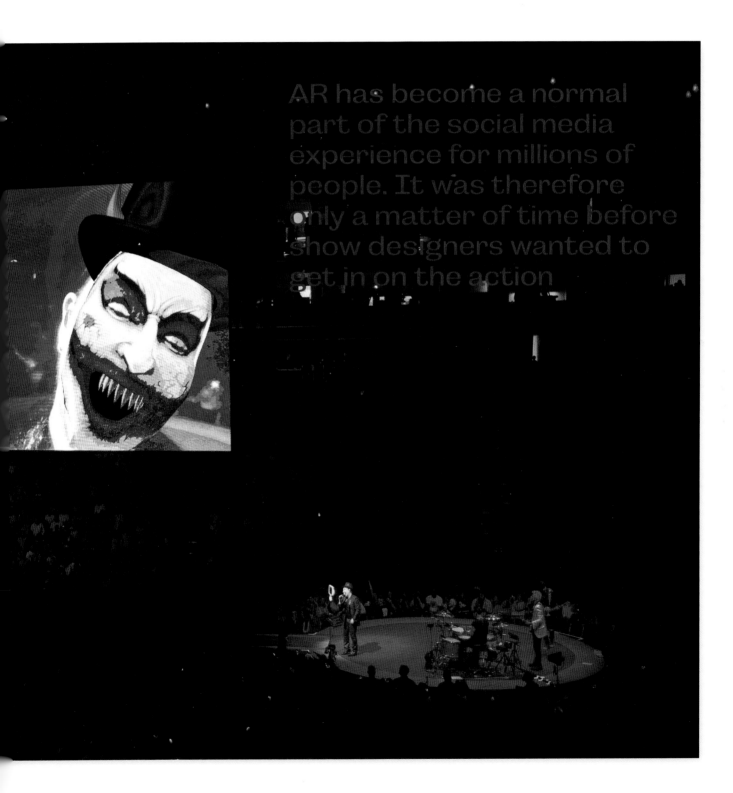

AR has become a normal part of the social media experience for millions of people. It was therefore only a matter of time before show designers wanted to get in on the action

STUFISH, Willie Williams and Es Devlin Studio,
U2 'eXPERIENCE + iNNOCENCE' world tour,
Tulsa, Oklahoma,
May 2018

Mr MacPhisto was originally a character in the 1992 'Zoo TV' show where Bono would paint his face with makeup. This resurrection in 2018 applies a digital makeup. STUFISH worked with Facebook and the Reality Augmented Studio company to create a bespoke digital filter that allowed Bono to transform himself, live. A camera was incorporated into a mirror that he could look into and be augmented. The signal was then projected onto the large screen. An example of AR technology being used in a live show as a storytelling device.

the content before the show, which makes it a minority experience; at least until '5G' networking rides in over the hill.

In the meantime, screen-based AR is more common. By tracking the position of the live camera, and rendering the virtual scene from its perspective, the designer can create virtual objects, lights and effects, or even virtual performers – as seen in Madonna's 'Billboards' performance in 2019 – which appear superimposed onto the camera feed.

Extended reality (also called mixed reality, or xR) goes a step further, rendering 3D content onto the LED screens *behind* the performer, as well as in front of them, allowing the designer to transport the performer into a virtual environment. Most famously embraced by acts such as Katy Perry, Billie Eilish and Arashi (2020), xR has a disruptive effect on how designers think about stage design. Rather than build elaborate physical worlds that have to be transported and rebuilt for each show, they can now build those worlds virtually and take us through many worlds in each show, rather as pop videos do.

This means that the roles of the stage designer and content creator now start to intersect. This requires designers to get to grips with a totally new design vocabulary, and to find new ways of integrating virtual designs with physical ones. As the industry adjusts to these disruptions, however, we can expect to see xR become a standard feature of live shows.

Virtually Real
Virtual reality (VR) places a tiny screen in front of each of your eyes and redraws the content as you move your head to trick your brain into feeling like you are

STUFISH,
Arashi 'This Is ARASHI LIVE 2020.12.31',
Tokyo Dome, Tokyo,
31 December 2020

This show, designed by STUFISH, was for live-stream only. A complex and giant multi-levelled physical stage was created that was constantly enhanced with additional in-camera AR effects, often blurring the line between what was real and what was virtual. The show design also had a specific area for an extended reality (xR) performance to be filmed.

isguise,
R stage,
ondon,
020

bove: The extended reality (xR) stage is designed to blend
rtual and physical worlds together using augmented reality
nd mixed reality to create fully immersive experiences. This
nage shows an example of the physical setup with position-
acked cameras and an LED wall and floor.

elow: Pre-visualisation in the Disguise media server
nowing an example of the virtual setup with a curved LED
creen and position-tracked camera that distorts the image
n the video screen to match the camera view in relation to
e performer and the bench.

somewhere else. Current VR is crude and blocky, but the technology is advancing quickly; by some estimates, we are fewer than five years away from true 'retina display' quality. If you think smartphones are dangerously addictive, you are going to *love* VR.

The solipsistic nature of VR makes it the diametric opposite of the heady communal experience of the live show. However, because VR immerses you completely in the content, it has the power to affect your emotions in a visceral, physiological way that a flat screen cannot. This makes it ideal as an extension to, rather than a replacement for, live shows. Imagine strategically placing live spherical video cameras in the crowd at a live concert and streaming those feeds out to the Internet. Suddenly your virtual audience can experience almost exactly what the real crowd does, but everyone gets to be in the front row. And since the stream is virtual, the show designer is free to enhance it in any way they choose. Suddenly, it becomes possible for Madonna to play her 'Madame X' theatre show, but to reach an audience of millions with just a few dates.

Life is a Cabaret

Live music, of course, is about more than just maximising ticket revenue. On a basic human level, live shows are where you go to discover, and be a part of, your tribe. To succeed, virtual 'gigs' will have to find a way of replicating this function. Imagine a virtual show experience where not only do you have a front-row seat, but you are surrounded by a dozen of your best friends and a smattering of friends-of-friends who like the same music. You can watch the show together, chat with anyone you want, and still see and hear the millions of fans around you (but with a convenient volume control).

Turn on your webcams and your video avatar gets streamed to the stage, so you could end up in the show, or even interact with the star if they choose you. Throw in a couple of (presumably handsomely compensated) celebrities nearby, and you have a pretty compelling package.

Since the stream is virtual, in fact, it is quite possible for the format to be personalised. So you could watch the show alone, or with your mum who lives on the other side of the world. You could invite your friends round for a 'viewing party', or you could watch together at the local cinema, with proper ribcage-rattling sound. Better still, all of these formats could co-exist simultaneously.

Virtual technologies cannot, and will not, replace live shows. Instead they offer new ways of including fans of all kinds in the experience, not just those who can travel to shows. So if you are that shy kid shut away with your PlayStation 10, virtual concerts might be just the spur you need to come and find out what this 'reality' is all about.⍙

Haidy Geismar

STUFISH,
Queen + Adam Lambert
'Rhapsody' world tour,
Seoul, South Korea,
January 2020

The synchronised images on the crowd's phones show a heart. This was not organised by the band; the decision by the crowd to unify under this image was completely spontaneous, and is an interesting example of one of the choreographic aspects of social media.

Curating the Crowd

Social Media and the Choreography of Affective Experience

The advent of social media and the ever more sophisticated functionality of our mobile phones have had a profound effect on the way we view and record events. This is particularly true for large gatherings of people. **Haidy Geismar**, Professor of Anthropology at University College London, explains how it was once possible to 'choreograph' an audience, but nowadays the audience choreographs itself, with thousands of simultaneous viewpoints that are disseminated in multiple, personal yet often public ways.

The history of entertainment architecture is also the history of curating the crowd – creating an experience for ever larger audiences that must balance the size of the venue (and the need to fill it) with the desire to make a visceral and embodied experience and enduring memory for each attendee. The history of 20th-century crowds and spectacle is also linked to that of cinema and visual media – in which the experience of 'being there' has long been mediated by screen technologies. The German philosopher and cultural critic Walter Benjamin, witnessing the turn towards fascism within Europe in the 1930s, recognised the power of cinema to harness political charisma and channel social movements by resituating the audience from being passive spectators to becoming active participants in popular events. For Benjamin, the aura of artworks in the age of mechanical reproduction gave way to the aura of the crowd, described evocatively by Elias Canetti in his sweeping survey *Crowds and Power* as an irresistible shared density of human experience.[1]

The anthropologist and historian of cinema Alison Griffiths has shown how technologies of immersion and interaction have shaped the spectacular experience within entertainment architecture from the medieval cathedral through to 19th-century panoramas and eventually to IMAX cinemas.[2] Whilst Griffiths focuses on how museums attempt to balance the pleasures of immersion with the need to be educational, her broader point is, like that of Benjamin, that screens are not 'outside of' or 'detached from' cultural production, nor do they inculcate passive viewing experiences, but rather are intrinsic tools in the active search for ever more 'real' and authentic embodied experiences. Following Griffiths's discussion of the experience of spectacular performance, this article explores the impact of social media in shifting the experience of the crowd from a singular moment into an embodied experience that is dispersed through time and space.

Designing for Social Media

Social media, even with the reorientation away from a wide-screen format towards the square boxes of Instagram, has domesticated the cinematic experience of spectacular performance, shifting the location of the image from that of a shared panorama to that of a shared and circulated digital file. Where the crowd was once understood as a mass of bodies, it is now a mass of signs: images, likes, comments, tags. But this should not mislead us to think that social media is a disembodied experience, or that it acts as a distancing device in the context of large-scale mass events. The anthropologist Paolo Gerbaudo has described social media as 'choreographic', exploring how platforms such as Twitter are used to mobilise crowds of political activists in the streets.[3] And in more intimate research, anthropologists have explored how smartphones facilitate a new form of co-presence with studies of how, for instance, migrant women parent their children through mobile phones whilst working overseas.[4] Nick Couldry has discussed how 'liveness' as a form of 'continued connectedness' can be mediated through online platforms, which both extend live connections between people who are not physically co-located and also extend this experience beyond the initial moment of performance.[5]

In the stadium, social media introduces new opportunities for design, in which screens increasingly become the focal point of the performance. Alongside the massification of the screen-based experience, large-scale concert design now also makes explicit use of the pocket-sized screens of smartphones and the social media platforms that they support – not just by switching from cigarette lighters to smartphone flashlights, but by designing 'Instagrammable' moments, and using audience recording as a form of choreography for the event, in which 'people not only film the screen that they are watching, they also film

FIRST APPEARANCE OF JENNY LIND IN AMERICA
At Castle Garden Sept. 11 1850

First appearance of
Jenny Lind in America,
at Castle Garden,
Battery Park,
New York,
11 September 1850

Jenny Lind was one of the world's most admired 19th-century singers. Her American tour during 1850–52 elicited such demand for tickets that they were sold by auction, and she provoked such enthusiasm that the phenomenon was called 'Lind Mania' by the press. The receipts totalled $26,238.

themselves watching the screen, and then go home and put that on Instagram because they want to be seen to have been at the event.'[6]

Describing the process of designing the Arashi concert at the Tokyo Dome on 31 December 2020, STUFISH Design Director and CEO Ray Winkler explains the salience of social media imagery both to the studio's design thinking, and to the client's experience of the design process, especially during the Covid-19 pandemic which pretty much stopped all mass events around the world. Speaking in January 2021, he commented: 'The experience now, at least in the last year, which has been very much driven by the virtual experience ... has brought in a very different way of thinking about these shows, and that is when we start thinking about the "Instagram moment", something that is there primarily to be seen through a very particular format.'[7]

Model of the structure of the touring stage showing the stage from the right, with the dual parallel runways that extend outwards from the main stage into the audience.

STUFISH,
Beyoncé and Jay-Z 'On the Run II' tour,
2018

Render showing the stage from the left. The runways extending into the audience maximised the potential for the performers to interact with the audience at a closer range, also allowing for better smartphone photographs and videos.

In the stadium, social media introduces new opportunities for design, in which screens increasingly become the focal point of the performance

STUFISH,
Mumford & Sons 'Delta' tour,
Belfast,
2018

The photograph shows the in-the-round stage,
designed to allow the band to be close-up with
more of the audience. See-through gauze projection
screens show live images of both the band and
the surrounding audience, further enhancing the
participatory experience.

As STUFISH progressed the design for the Arashi show, Winkler described how social media was not simply a fix for Covid-appropriate design, but actually became integral to the design process itself, as STUFISH worked remotely with the client: 'It was all seen through the camera lens and the interesting thing is our process which starts with a conversation followed by reference images, which is then followed by sketches which is then followed by 3D models, you can absolutely see the trajectory of the idea manifesting itself into one that looks really good on camera because it has to look really good on the computer screen when you present this to your artist, who is sitting in Japan in front of a computer screen, looking at that very image, and you know that that very image is going to be replicated on millions of people's screens because it is exactly the same format that you designed this in, which is a very interesting loop.'[8]

Extending Time and Space

Even more strikingly than the, by now common, imagery of people using phones as flashlights, or to record (and broadcast) their own version of an event, are the ways in which smartphones can extend the moment or time of an experience outwards across a prolonged temporal, and spatial, arc. Many assume that the remediation of a concert through the mobile phone of the fan is an act of distancing, shifting the sensory experience of 'being there' to one of watching a less visceral on-screen performance. It is however clear that this extendable form of remediation also creates intensely embodied and participatory experiences.

In my own research into the digitisation of museum collections it is becoming clear that processes of digitisation have been used by cultural groups to create new histories and forms of profound connection to historic objects. In the case of *Te Ara Wairua*, a 2014 project to digitise a Māori cloak held in the Ethnography Collections of University College London (UCL), rather than seeing digital images of the cloak as less authentic, these digital experiences were framed as containers of the same spiritual energy and capacities for connection (*wairua*) that the original treasure (*taonga*) was imbued with. By creating a virtual environment, the project transformed the Octagon Gallery at UCL into a sacred and ceremonial Māori space, likened to the forecourt in front of a Māori meeting house, the *marae ātea*. Within this reversal, employees of UCL and members of the London Māori Club, Ngāti Rānana, were welcomed as guests by Te Matahiapo Indigenous Research Organisation, broadcasting from the base of Mount Taranaki in the North Island, and the cloak was bathed in light and sound from Aotearoa (the Māori name for New Zealand). The project, and the subsequent discussion it sparked amongst its participants,[9] shows how digital platforms may be understood in practice not as less authentic simulacra of reality, but as important channels for social and cultural experiences. This argument is an important cornerstone of the growing field of digital anthropology.[10]

In the arena, as the singular moment of the concert is now refracted through a million user accounts, endlessly circulated through YouTube videos and Instagram clips, the opportunity for direct engagement may also be increased. For instance, in the Arashi concert, whilst the group played to an empty stadium due to the constraints of the Covid-19 pandemic, live streams of images from the Instagram feeds of millions of spectators were projected into the arena, and onto the stage, which in turn was remediated through the screens of the watching participants. This was deliberately part of the design process, as described by Ray Winkler: 'the purpose of the event in itself has changed from being a deeply personal one that you share maybe with a handful of people at most within the context of a crowd of 100,000 people to sharing it with millions of people'. He went on: 'When there were no crowds in the stadium because of social distancing … we had never received more likes to our design at

STUFISH,
Arashi 'This Is ARASHI LIVE 2020.12.31',
Tokyo Dome,
Tokyo,
31 December 2020

For live-stream only, the set was designed from London during lockdown and built in Japan for the New Year's concert. Conceived specifically to be viewed by an online audience while the band played in an empty stadium, this rendering shows The Solar Farm – a large mirror ball that descended and split apart to reveal the band inside to begin the show. An array of 72 radial LED screens on kinetic arms streamed live images of fans' faces from their Instagram feeds.

Live streams of images from the Instagram feeds of millions of spectators were projected into the arena, and onto the stage, which in turn was remediated through the screens of the watching participants

STUFISH,
U2 'eXPERIENCE + iNNOCENCE' world tour,
2018

A photo of the U2 tour, showing how the audience could use their phones and a custom-made U2 smartphone app to create AR (augmented reality) images and videos superimposed over the live performance in front of them. An AR avatar of Bono is shown 'looming' over the audience.

STUFISH,
Arashi 'This Is ARASHI
LIVE 2020.12.31',
Tokyo Dome,
Tokyo,
31 December 2020

The Arashi Vortex. XR (extended reality) technology, which allows virtual and physical worlds to be blended together in live production environments, was used to create an impressive digital layer over the physical set within the Tokyo Dome.

that moment because everyone experienced the show through the lens through which it was designed, and that was a visually beautiful composed piece of stage architecture that people could experience on a screen.'[11]

This design intention was borne out by the response of the viewers, as in the case of one blogger's review of the show where they recount the intensity of their viewing experience of this final concert in some detail: 'I do remember the little moments … i was fighting back tears as i was striving to catch every single word they said and not miss any single micro-expression they showed through and through, as if i tried to burn those images onto my brain forever.'[12]

The crowd, and the sense of being there, is now dispersed across time, and prolonged in an ongoing and participatory curation of both public and private memory. The scale of the smartphone paradoxically now makes live stadium performances seem small. In some ways, curating the crowd is about managing the tensions between the physical experience of 'being there' and the optics of being able to experience the event in an enduring way over time. As Walter Benjamin so presciently observed, the advent of mass media allows for the transformation of the audience into what he describes as 'the critic'.[13] Even writing in the age of analogue media, Benjamin recounted how readers were becoming writers, and audiences were becoming directors, cinematographers, photographers and actors within their own spectacles. Social media continues, and intensifies, this trajectory. Perhaps this is most viscerally encountered by the ways in which a mass event like a stadium concert, when seen through the lens of a smartphone, is experienced as much discursively as visually – evinced by the importance of comments, likes and tags alongside images within social media platforms. Whilst Benjamin was interested in exploring the capacity of mass media to enable (and disable) political action, today's mass entertainment events are also opening up profound questions about the form and experience of cultural memory. They expose some of the ways in which scale and value are entwined, and also pose problems for each other. The questions for post-Covid entertainment architectures are both about how to create enduring cultural experiences, and how to manage their ownership. Questions over the authority and power of the 'fan', the ways in which their value is spatialised in the largest-scale events, and the role of smartphone technology in mediating this are becoming vital components of the design process. ∆

Notes
1. Walter Benjamin, 'The Work of Art in the Age of Mechanical Reproduction' [1936], in *Illuminations*, Fontana (London), 1992, pp 211–44; Elias Canetti, *Crowds and Power* [originally published in German as *Masse und Macht*, 1960], Penguin (Harmondsworth), 1984.
2. Alison Griffiths, *Shivers Down Your Spine: Cinema, Museums, and the Immersive View*, Columbia University Press (New York), 2008.
3. Paolo Gerbaudo, *Tweets and the Streets: Social Media and Contemporary Activism*, Pluto Press (London), 2012.
4. Mirca Madianou and Daniel Miller, 'Mobile Phone Parenting: Reconfiguring Relationships between Filipina Migrant Mothers and Their Left-Behind Children', *New Media & Society*, 13 (3), 2011, pp 457–70: https://doi.org/10.1177/1461444810393903.
5. Nick Couldry, 'Liveness, "Reality", and the Mediated Habitus from Television to the Mobile Phone', *The Communication Review*, 7 (4), 2004, pp 353–61.
6. Author interview with Ric Lipson, STUFISH, 8 January 2021.
7. Author interview with Ray Winkler, STUFISH, 8 January 2021.
8. *Ibid*.
9. See Haidy Geismar, *Museum Object Lessons for the Digital Age*, UCL Press (London), 2018, Chapter 6.
10. Daniel Miller, 'Digital Anthropology', in Felix Stein *et al.* (eds), *The Cambridge Encyclopedia of Anthropology*, 2018: www.anthroencyclopedia.com/entry/digital-anthropology.
11. Author interview with Ray Winkler, STUFISH, 8 January 2021.
12. 'Goodally', 'This is 嵐 LIVE: The Music Never Ends' blog, 10 January 2021: https://bean5spilled.wordpress.com/2021/01/10/this-is-嵐-live-the-music-never-ends/.
13. Benjamin, *op cit*, p 221.

Adam Davis

SPIRALLING INTO PERFECTION

STAGING THE CHOREOGRAPHY OF PORTABILITY

What is important is to understand and circumvent the many parameters that determine the success of a touring show. These can include modularity, ergonomics, language of assemblers and expedient durability amongst many other issues. **Adam Davis** is Chief Creative Officer of TAIT – the architectural engineering and software company that has worked with everyone from Elton John to Beyoncé and U2. He explains TAIT's 'design spiral' approach and the benefits of collaborative creative processes.

STUFISH (built by TAIT),
AC/DC 'Rock or Bust' world tour,
2015-16

This panoramic preshow image in Arnhem's GelreDome football stadium in the Netherlands shows the scale of the loading-in process of the entire set for the stadium tour. The main stage is being built on the left, showing the steel roof structure clad in custom scenic 'industrial-looking' fascia with incorporated LED lighting. In the centre is one of the trucks used for the load-in.

The touring entertainment industry is one of the most incredible places to work as a designer and problem-solver because there are very few creative or technical limitations and a host of unique challenges to solve.

During the process of designing a car, much will already be known: it will have wheels and some sort of power transmission. Similarly, a plane will have wings and a house will have bathrooms. But when designing and creating the structures and technology for live events, the opposite is true, and there are time constraints to everything. When artists are added to the equation – challenging you to do something new, amazing and unprecedented for them – there is an inevitable drive to innovate from the ground up, because of those ever-present time constraints and other complexities unique to the entertainment industry.

Then there are logistical considerations. For example, every city a tour visits might have a team of people that speaks a different language. Some of them may not have seen the equipment before. Thirty trucks of equipment might need to be emptied and loaded in, with everything set up for the show inside eight hours. Then afterwards everything needs to be loaded out into those same 30 trucks in four hours. These sorts of challenges make this industry the ideal arena for driving real creativity and innovation.

Over the years, to cope with these circumstances, TAIT has invented a process of innovation based around concurrent design and manufacture. During the traditional design process, something is sketched out, engineered, the material procured and then manufactured, tested and assembled. Each element must happen consecutively. At TAIT we have a non-linear approach to design, called 'the design spiral', which is about identifying the boundary conditions and constraints of a project.

For highway-department engineers designing a bridge, the constraints and conditions that control the processes are very different to those of the touring world. In designing infrastructure for the touring world, the goal is not to create something that will withstand a hundred years of repetitive use. It is about making sure it is possible to organise the logistics of getting all the necessary parts and pieces set up within the required timescale and figuring out how long is needed to work with them, and then what the scheduling limitations are. The design spiral allows TAIT's design team to quickly identify all the constraints that must be taken into consideration, and subsequently which ones need to be prioritised.

These constraints are always different depending on the time frame, where the tour is going, the engineering and packaging requirements, and whether the tour will be flown all over the world versus a one-off local event. Because every project is different, design teams are unable to apply the same process and priority tools every time.

Prototype, Prototype, Prototype

In traditional manufacturing, there is almost zero flexibility. The operation must be made as lean as possible, so that the same thing happens every time with the minimum excess in terms of time, cost and materials. In contrast, TAIT embraces the idea that some creative routes simply will not work. But when ideas are discarded because they have led the design team to the next thing, it is not considered a waste of time. It is necessary to understand that the creative design process is an iterative journey; there will be failure along the way to get to something brilliant at the end.

When working with STUFISH, for example, they will often bring a rock star's concept for their stage show to the design table. More often than not, the technology to realise that concept and make it work does not exist yet. So initial brainstorming sessions often begin with 'What is the most outlandish way of doing this?' and 'What is a way of doing this that no one would consider possible?' This leads to a discussion about things like inflatables, springs or magnets. A very important part of the process, both at TAIT and STUFISH, is a lack of egotism – being generous about adding ideas to the mix without being afraid to have those ideas rejected. Before the plan is executed, all the different strategies that could be used to solve a problem are considered to establish which is the most effective.

STUFISH (built by TAIT),
Michael Bublé 'An Evening with Michael Bublé' world tour,
2019–21

View from backstage during load-in, showing the back of the automated curved video screen that rises and descends throughout the performance. The multi-levelled orchestra stand in front of it incorporates a central lift for Bublé's entrance and integrated lighting effects. The underside of the structure becomes a densely packed technical support area for the show.

First and foremost, that means gathering a multidisciplinary team and taking the time to make sure everybody is laser-focused on the goal. That goal might be to make something that can be set up in four hours, but that can also fit in an aeroplane, and then transfer to a sea container, and finally deliver the 'wow' experience to audiences.

It is vital to work through what the goal is and then focus on the criteria. The design team does not spend its time debating the final decision, but the criteria that will be used to make the decision. If that is done right, the decision actually becomes very easy.

Once the goal is established, the focus shifts to a thorough discussion of what criteria will be used to make the strategy decisions. Then the team considers what the parameters are. In design, people often go straight to the plan; skipping strategy, they say, 'Ok, I understand the goal – I've done this before'. TAIT tries to take as much time as needed to debate all the different potential approaches.

As various constraints and ways forward are evaluated, the benefits of working with a cross-functional team with different specialties, instead of just having engineers working through a problem at their desks, become evident. This often leads the team to a process that TAIT calls 'prototype, prototype, prototype', as opposed to 'God design' where the ethos is more 'I'm a genius engineer and I'm going to figure it out perfectly and just go and build it'.

STUFISH,
Willie Williams and Es Devlin Studio (built by TAIT),
U2 'eXPERIENCE + iNNOCENCE' world tour,
2015

above: The inside of the 'Barricage' during construction. The double-sided see-through video screen with an interior walkway was positioned down the centre of the arena for performances. The large structure could be raised and lowered, and had integrated lighting and automated lifting sections that allowed the band to be revealed within.

STUFISH (built by TAIT),
Lady Gaga 'Born This Way Ball'
world tour,
2012–13

right: This image from the TAIT workshop in Lititz, Pennsylvania, shows the assembly and integration of a large-scale multi-level structure that was embellished to look like a stone castle. The different levels were assembled on the ground and then lifted into place. Parts of the complex design were automated to have moving walls, stairs, opening windows and integrated lighting.

At the centre of the stage designed and fabricated by TAIT was a large, complex and heavy piece of stage automation nicknamed 'The Machine', here shown in TAIT's workshop. This structure could lift 12 performers to a height of 10 feet (3 metres), and rotate from flat on the stage to vertical and any angle in between to enable the show's various choreographed elements.

TAIT's approach is, 'Let's go and build our first object as quickly as possible and learn what we don't know about it.'

Embracing Experimentation

TAIT believes it is much more efficient to have a sandbox in which to experiment. The firm's approach is, 'Let's go and build our first object as quickly as possible and learn what we don't know about it.' Then the fabricators and procurement experts are brought around the table to help the design team understand how it can be improved, and then more prototyping takes place.

The company has found that rather than taking the time to design and engineer something perfectly, much better results are achieved in a much shorter time period by embracing the design dead-ends and the experimentation that come with prototyping over and over, before finally locking in something that the team *knows* is the best solution.

And that is the idea with the design spiral – it is a process of spiralling into perfection. It is not a linear process where one decision is made, and the next, and the next. One per cent of every decision is made, and then the second per cent is made, and then the third and so on until, by the time the process has been completed, every decision is at 100 per cent effectively refining the way to perfection.

Once the wider team understands how TAIT works, and the fabrication and machine-shop leads have already been included in a design review about the best way to solve the problem, everyone is already on board with the approach. This means that rather than handing over a complete design package with all the specs and plans before going to production, the production team is already up to speed because they have been part of the design process. So internally TAIT is very efficient, in that an electronic file can be sent to the machine shop and they can make an immediate start, which massively accelerates the fabrication time.

left: Onstage view of the video flippers in a staggered formation. On the surfaces of the screens, images of smoke and colour appear to create a dynamic background to the performance. The flippers were reflected in the highly polished floor to create a bigger and more seamless look.

opposite: TAIT created the stage set's 13 one-of-a-kind automated video 'flippers', integrated into the main stage to provide a complex, fluid, moving LED display. The flippers could be individually sequenced to move to any angle and up to 90 degrees in 4 seconds. This view looks into the supporting structure and across the back of the mechanics.

Trust the Process

Unlike in the world of fixed-installation construction, where everything needs to be 100 per cent decided before it is cast in concrete and steel, in the portable touring world there is a tendency – also on the part of the entertainers – to gravitate towards working teams that have been together for years, that have been through the process over and over again, so not everything needs to be figured out in order to take a jump with the confidence something great will result from the team effort.

TAIT fabricates a large proportion of the shows STUFISH designs. For Madonna's 'Rebel Heart' tour (2015–16), STUFISH collaborated with the artist on the original staging concepts and design, then provided the specifications and design intent TAIT followed when building all of the staging, props and automated rigging elements. Throughout the process of creation and prototyping, TAIT and STUFISH were in constant communication confirming details and finishes, and sharing progress through photos and frequent shop visits.

On a global tour, moving around the world to hundreds of cities, attracting thousands and thousands of people, TAIT is accountable for delivering a set and staging experience that is authentic, true to the artist's vision, and that will send the audience home with lifelong memories. The trust the artist places in us is not taken lightly, so arguably the most important item on the checklist is having a crew that can be relied upon to deliver the goods. When producing a show there will inevitably be pivots and experiments during the process of getting to opening night with something truly brilliant as the output, just as TAIT has done for years and years, project after project.

Live-show image taken at the point of the pyrotechnics explosion. The true scale of the design fabricated by TAIT is referenced against the mass of audience with magnified images shown on the large incorporated side screens.

Once everyone understands what is required, an element of the project will be taken and optimised, to try to make sure the whole group can succeed, and that becomes a design spiral. The project will be broken into elements and each element becomes a spiral. Each element will be taken and made into a kit – something on which a barcode can be put and tracked anywhere in the world – and that becomes a spiral. The kits are broken down into parts and they go through individual design spirals, and eventually we get to the complete and final criteria for each individual part.

This is a very sophisticated logistics challenge: tracking 10 million parts that all have to be made perfectly. There must be complete traceability along the entire manufacturing chain: where the material came from, who touched it every step of the way, exactly what machine it went onto and how many minutes it took to mill. TAIT has built a logistical backend that allows the company to deal with the complexity of having millions and millions of parts coming together in a choreographed dance in real time while concurrently designing and manufacturing to achieve the ultimate goal: creating a moment in people's lives they will never forget.

A Place for Everything
A casual observer watching a show being loaded in or out would not know that TAIT has choreographed every part of it. An observer of one of our design reviews would see the designer in front of the team acting out the process of 'How am I going to take it out of its cart?' 'How am I going to apply this component to the next component?' Because if five seconds can be saved at every step, the time saved adds up to hours by the time the load-in process has finished. It is about optimising every decision: 'Why is that 1/8th of an inch outside that hole and not 1/16th of an inch?' 'Why is that washer there?'

The team makes sure everything has a purpose and is part of a bigger dance that becomes the load-in process that makes these shows happen in front of the audience's eyes. In many ways it is a hidden art. Going backstage and seeing how the show is constructed is a show in itself, but one that only the crew are privileged enough to see.

The team at STUFISH has been a linchpin of many of TAIT's projects, most recently Elton John's 'Farewell Yellow Brick Road' tour (2018–23). We have worked together since the early 1990s and that brings a level of trust and vulnerability that allows us to push the boundaries together. Our collective job is to create these moments in space and time that 'wow' people, that change their lives in one way or other. At the other end of the spectrum is a creative process where trust, failure and vulnerability are embraced, and in the middle is the spiral of excellence where we are constantly striving to iterate our way to perfection. ⌂

CREATING PERFORMANCE ENVIRONMENTS

S. Leonard Auerbach

STUFISH and Auerbach Pollock Friedlander,
Dai Show Theatre,
Xishuangbanna, Yunnan province,
China,
2015

The audience is seated around a 1,400-square-metre (15,000-square-foot) stage split into three sections. The central stage spans 14 metres (46 feet), and is divided into a shallow pool area 0.3 metres (1 foot) deep and 8 metres (26 feet) wide, with a 5.5-metre (18-foot) deep pool in the middle which allows for dramatic high dives from the catwalk above. A proprietary computer-controlled video projection system designed by Auerbach Pollock Friedlander combined with the show's water effects to create a visually exciting performance.

TECHNOLOGY, DESIGN AND PATIENCE

S. Leonard Auerbach is Founder and Design Director of San Francisco–based Auerbach Pollock Friedlander (APF) who provide theatre and theatrical systems design and audio–video consulting services. He charts a series of creative interactions and collaborations with STUFISH from 2003 onwards that are highly architectural and theatrical, and international in their scope.

The genre of entertainment architecture encompasses a realm of venue types that have evolved over centuries of human communication, beginning with an individual, an audience and a place. The evolution of the performance space ranges from a public space or marketplace (agora) in which a person would voice an opinion for debate, to built venues responding to a playwright/philosopher, the Greek theatre and, eventually, architecture which facilitates every conceivable audience–performer relationship. Consequently, the development of entertainment architecture has sympathetically responded to artistic, social, political and technological demands. From the Greeks to Shakespeare, opera, Broadway, circus, rock and roll, cinema and audience-immersive environments, the work of STUFISH exemplifies a unique responsiveness to the broad spectrum of architectural and audience interactions of where we have been and where we are going.

Where We Have Been and Where We Are Going
We live in a changing world that presents new challenges in the arts, live performance entertainment and architecture. There has been a historical evolution of how we gather, communicate and express ourselves: beginning with the most primitive gatherings around a fire, storytelling, and drawing on cave walls, to presenting in front of natural features, building amphitheatres to enable scripted presentations and later adapting great halls and bear-baiting pits for performances, consequently leading to festival stages and Baroque music rooms. Theatre architecture evolved to become opera houses, sports arenas, civic auditoriums, show rooms, Broadway / West End theatres, repertory theatres, jazz joints, themed attraction venues, dark rides, popular entertainment spaces, rock-and-roll extravaganzas, outdoor festivals and audience-immersive environments. Advances in presentation technology enabled us to create architectural environments that respond to unlimited artistic expression. The practice of creating entertainment architecture now and in the future demands a keen approach to the architectural pathways we take.

Throughout history we have benefited from the talent and vision of architects, their clients, and patrons of the arts. We are now on a cusp of change that requires a collective effort from multi-discipline talent to respond to the next level of artistic expression. STUFISH functions as a team that has demonstrated the kind of architectural leadership which can guide us along the pathway to wherever our visions may take us.

First Encounters that Led the Way
In 2003 Auerbach Pollock Friedlander (APF) was finalising its first venue for Cirque du Soleil's production of *Zumanity* (2003–20) at MGM's New York-New York Hotel & Casino in Las Vegas. As the theatre consultant, APF had overcome the challenge of converting the existing New York-New York headliner show room into a Cirque du Soleil themed show theatre. The Director of MGM Design

Group had said that if this project were successful, the team would go across the street to the MGM Grand Hotel & Casino for another purpose-built show theatre. So on to MGM Grand and the introduction to Mark Fisher, founder of STUFISH and at the time the theatre architect and scenic designer for Cirque du Soleil's production of *KÀ*, completed in 2004.

The APF team have enjoyed the privilege of working with several world-renowned architects and the experience of knowing and working closely with Mark Fisher and STUFISH has been one of the greatest such pleasures. The challenge of converting the MGM Grand EFX theatre into the Cirque du Soleil *KÀ* theatre heralded a success that brought the practice into a design/consulting relationship with STUFISH which continued in Las Vegas for Cirque du Soleil's *Viva Elvis* (2010–12) and then to China with the Wanda Cultural Tourism Planning & Research Institute company.

STUFISH was well along with what was then called
Dalian Wanda Group's 2,000-seat Han Show Theatre
project in Wuhan, China (completed 2014) when APF
was asked to consult on their next venue, the 1,183-
seat Dai Show Theatre in Xishuangbanna in Yunnan
province (completed 2015). The show producer was
Franco Dragone Entertainment Group and the creative
aspect of the show had yet to be confirmed; the initial
criteria were simply that it would be a water show,
with a pool including a submerged stage lift and
extensive water effects.

It is not unusual that purpose-built theatres require
design and construction processes to be on different
timelines than the show production. Show theatres
require an accelerated design and construction process
to meet business demands, while the show's creative
team has yet to conceive or fully design the production

STUFISH,
Cirque du Soleil *VIVA Elvis* Theatre,
Aria Resort and Casino,
MGM CityCenter,
Paradise, Nevada,
2010

Early concept render. The vast stage is composed of multiple
stage lifts of varying sizes, performer lifts and mechanised
sliding platforms. These bring massive pieces of scenery onto
the stage for different scenes, and create the extensive, multi-
level staging flexibility needed to bring the spirit and energy
of Elvis's performances to life for a modern audience.

STUFISH and Auerbach Pollock Friedlander,
Dai Show Theatre,
Xishuangbanna,
Yunnan province,
China,
2015

STUFISH is a practice that encompasses the ability to deliver all the architectural, set and show elements for a theatre specifically designed for a production. The primary folding trusses of the roof shown in this aerial view are visible from inside the theatre, and the repetitive folding patterns can be seen through the entire theatre space, flowing into golden walls that merge with the ceiling, creating an intimate yet airy atmosphere. This STUFISH design concept was engineered by Atelier One.

SECTION A-A

1. EXTERNAL PUBLIC LOBBY
2. RETAIL
3. AUDITORIUM
4. CENTRAL HIGH DIVE POOL
5. SHALLOW POOL
6. DRAGON ROOT PROSCENIUM
7. DRY STAGE AREA
8. LIVE BAND PLATFORM
9. CONTROL ROOM
10. CATWALK
11. GRID

The set was specifically designed for a water acrobatic show, with ten acrobatic gates and an elaborate 3D flying system integrated into the design of the roof structure, allowing performers to take off from the 9-metre (30-foot) platform and soar above both the stage and the audience.

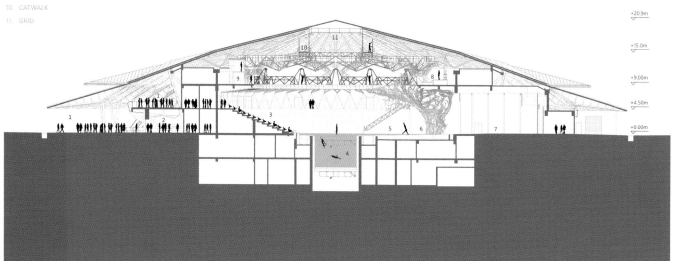

that the theatre must be designed for. This is not a situation where the show must fit into a pre-existing venue, but where the venue must be designed for a production that is intended to play for many years. In such cases APF takes on the role of enabler in the process of understanding the needs of the production and working with the architect to support an architectural parti that is essential to the design process.

It is critical that this process is respectful and harmonious in reaching everyone's goals. Mark Fisher enabled such harmony, and the results speak for themselves. He had a way of putting his talented staff in the forefront with the client and the consulting team and responding with clear direction and tone that brought out the best from everyone. Whereas in Las Vegas the high-pressure corporate casino world demanded a decisive manner to meet their needs, in China the clients were short on experience for such venues but aggressive in their vision, and the client corporate structure there was bound by a cultural hierarchy that fostered decision-making which evolved from a many-layered process, adding considerable time. The STUFISH team has always been able to navigate the cultural differences with a high level of artistic sensitivity and their patience and determination always set a tone of cohesiveness.

Process: The Demand for Groundbreaking Technology

During the design of themed and purpose-built theatres the challenge is to go beyond the existing technology to support the unique vision of the specific production. As production demands are developed, a clear understanding of the required physical armature for the stage technology and architectural direction can be established. As the production director, scenic designer, choreographer, technical director, lighting designer *et al* make their vision take form, the gauntlet is down for the theatre consultant to put the 'works' together. APF's way of working is to collaborate directly with the architect, construction teams and the production's creative team, and foster the production's technical requirements in terms that the owner best understands, thus securing a successful outcome.

Working with STUFISH has shown that the most challenging concepts can be achieved by re-imagining the theatrical technology. For millennia theatre technology has progressed at an ever-increasing pace, beginning with the *deus ex machina* of ancient Greece, where actors playing gods were brought onto stage using a trapdoor or crane. It evolved to use ships' windlass rigging, slot stages, hemp fly systems (so called because of the hemp ropes used), counterweight flying, hydraulic lifts, limelight, saltwater dimmers (which used salinity and distance between metal contacts to control the brightness of the lamp), resistance dimmers, vacuum tube remote-controlled dimmers, solid-state dimming, video imaging and the technology that is moving us towards a future in which we may create any visual and immersive

show or audience environment imaginable. With the theatrical industry no longer bound by old traditional 'barnyard technology', designers are able to embrace high-tech industry developments from electronics to manufacturing. The ability to provide expertise with practitioners from every theatre discipline, rather than academic theorists, has proved to be highly successful when collaborating with STUFISH, and *KÀ* is a pertinent example.

Mark Fisher's concept for the 'Sand Cliff Deck' gantry was first expressed in his early sketches. APF needed to understand the aesthetic and physical performance requirements of this key element as it would need to fit into the existing building structure. Development progressed with plans by McLaren Engineers for the gantry's hydraulics and structure. The gantry is a 25 × 60-foot (8 × 18-metre) travelling stage element that weighs 280,000 pounds (127,000 kilograms), with a structural framework of 8 feet (2.4 metres) containing special effects and performer access and enabling changing deck conditions with all machinery, lighting and theatrical elements accommodated within the

STUFISH,
Cirque du Soleil *KÀ* stage,
MGM Grand,
Las Vegas, Nevada,
2005

STUFISH founder Mark Fisher's early sketch of the Cirque du Soleil *KÀ* stage shows that from the beginning, the concept dispensed with a conventional stage with a permanent floor. Performers work across moving platforms that cantilever out over the void where the stage floor would ordinarily be, appearing to float through bottomless space.

The *KÀ* Sand Cliff Deck was used throughout the show, becoming a ship, a cliff and a sandy beach – the sand simulated by granular cork. Eighty steel pegs hidden within the deck can be individually triggered to provide handholds for the acrobats. It was the largest of two major automated stages and eight smaller ones used during the production. These earned *KÀ* the prestigious Thea Award for Outstanding Technical Achievement in 2008.

On enquiring how close to the people in the first row of the audience the deck needed to be, the response from STUFISH was that, ideally, the performers would be able to serve drinks to them

During the Battle scene, the Sand Cliff Deck tilted to become vertical, and performers 'fought' on its touch-sensitive grid surface, which interacted with a video projection system to create virtual ripples around their footsteps. The changing geometry of the platform plays with the audience's perceptions of space and allowed the performers to seemingly defy gravity.

structural framework. It travels from 30 feet (9 metres) below stage to 40 feet (12 metres) above stage at a speed of 2 feet (0.6 metre) per second, rotates 360 degrees and tilts from flat to 110 degrees vertically. The deck surface is embedded with a touch-sensitive grid that interacts with a video projection system responding to acrobatic dancers' contact, affecting the image and creating wave effects. A beach sand topping is provided by granular cork pellets that are spilled off the deck when it tilts and other effects are produced. The hydraulic lifting system utilises 4,000 US gallons (15,000 litres) of hydraulic fluid through four 70-foot (21-metre) long hoisting shafts. On enquiring how close to the people in the first row of the audience the deck needed to be, the response from STUFISH was that, ideally, the performers would be able to serve drinks to them. After detailed design coordination with the structural engineer of the executive architects (Marnell Corrao Associates), APF paired the gantry to work spatially with five surrounding high-speed stage lifts, a slip stage, electro-mechanical overhead rigging and 3D travelling acrobatic hoists and special effects. The design documentation for such efforts must be highly conformed amongst all architectural and show disciplines such as structure, MEP (mechanical, electrical and plumbing), HVAC (heating, ventilation and air conditioning), special effects and life safety.

A critical part of the process for major elements such as the gantry is factory testing, where the major elements are completely built, tested, modified and disassembled to be shipped to the project site. This enables efficient installation rather than building on-site where construction conditions and time are factors. The gantry mechanism was built and tested in Canada prior to shipment. Six different engineering specialists worked on the various controls, hydraulics, piping and interface with other show run systems. The success of this unique and outstanding technical achievement is largely the result of STUFISH's broad experience in rock

The gantry mechanism during installation. Auerbach Pollock Friedlander collaborated on rigging, stage lifts and machinery, lighting, sound, and automation control for the stage lifts and floating deck. The customised vertical gantry crane controlling the Sand Cliff Deck is essentially a giant robotic arm attached to four 75-foot (23-metre) long hydraulic cylinders running along two support columns. The deck's power is provided by five 50-horsepower pumps and a 4,000-US-gallon (15,000-litre) oil reservoir.

and roll and in the design of other grand performance environments such as the U2 and Pink Floyd arena shows, Queen Victoria Memorial stage at Buckingham Palace for Her Majesty the Queen's Diamond Jubilee in 2012, and the Opening and Closing Ceremonies for the 2008 Beijing Olympic Games.

A Timeline to be Understood

The pathway of development for an architectural project is unlike anything highly experienced individuals from the show side of theatre may have experienced in mounting a stage production. It is important to make sure everyone collaborating on a project understands the comparison in terms professional and personal gratification.

Traditional productions have a relatively short timeline of four to six months from beginning to opening. Once the audition has been won or someone is hired, the pleasure and enthusiasm aroused by meeting the creative team and learning the scope of the production a few weeks later gives way to great energy during the six- to 10-week design and rehearsal period. Mounting and rehearsing the production in the theatre takes another three to five weeks, after which the production opens to 'instant' gratification and much celebration.

Major theatre building projects have a potential timeline of four to six *years*. The time between responding to an RFP (request for proposal) and being awarded an interview is five to 10 weeks. The pleasure and enthusiasm aroused by kick-off and engagement in a three- to four-month concept and programming phase with the creative team must be maintained through another three- to four-month schematic design phase, plus two months for additional design changes, before the pleasure of design approval. Design development takes three to four months, plus another two months for cost reduction, before the relief of beginning the construction documents. Four to five months later more relief is felt at being able to get them out to bid. Some 24 to 30 months of construction administration follow – including bid review, submittals, site visits, factory acceptance testing and final commissioning and testing – before handover to the user. Production moves in, and after four months of rehearsal the opening takes place. Now, and only now, can the team feel the full gratification of a completed project, celebrate, feel the show and the audience.

It takes a certain kind of dedication to work on one theatre architecture project for four to five years to celebrate its success, compared to five to six months on a production opening in an existing venue.

Over the years the STUFISH team have shown themselves able to maintain a high level of quality and spirit in every one of their projects APF has experienced, and in their relationships with all disciplines imbedded in entertainment architecture. ∆

Text © 2021 John Wiley & Sons Ltd. Images: pp 82–3 © STUFISH, photo Raphael Olivier; pp 84–7 © STUFISH; p 88(t) © Nils Becker; p 88(b) © Tom Muscionico/Cirque du Soleil; p 89 © Auerbach Pollock Friedlander

STUFISH,
Cirque du Soleil *KÀ* stage,
MGM Grand,
Las Vegas, Nevada,
2005

This initial sketch by Mark Fisher of the *KÀ*
lobby and auditorium treatment is influenced
by the palisade of tree trunks that supports the
Kiyomizu-dera temple (1633) in Kyoto, Japan.

MAciej Woroniecki

THE INTRICATE ARCHITECTURE OF ENCHANTMENT

STUFISH partner **MAciej Woroniecki** explains some of the parameters that entertainment architects need to consider. They include aspects such as the definition of the brief, the materiality of the proposition, its programmatic appropriateness, its portability and weight and its cost. Above all there must be a clear project narrative that drives the special and spectacular.

As an established profession, architecture is a relatively modern concept, but the profession has an evolutionary history that can be traced back to Greek antiquity, and the man-made wonders of the world, both ancient and modern, are architectural creations.

The architectural process can pull cities back from the brink of collapse but can also be a contributing factor to the slow decay of a once great metropolis. To become an active participant in the moulding of the built environment is an attractive prospect for a young and ambitious mind. It quickly becomes clear to the budding architect, however, that the study and practice of architecture involves every discipline under the sun. Very quickly the scope of study expands to include biology, philosophy, mechanical and structural engineering, coding and even the culinary arts. I recall STUFISH founder Mark Fisher once saying in a brief and direct design review crit, 'An architect should know everything.' While this may be impossible, the architect must try to know something, at least, about everything.

As their studies progress, students begin to focus their interests. However, regardless of which of the many approaches to architectural design a student eventually chooses, to successfully affect the built environment and those inhabiting it, the student must have had a rigorous, comprehensive education and practical experience, whichever architectural school they have attended. Arguably, this is particularly true in the entertainment sector, as most of the projects have a condensed timeline and are a crash course in the architectural process. Nevertheless, what makes entertainment architecture unique among the other kinds of architecture is the narrative-driven blending of structure, stage, audience and performance into a lasting memory for global audiences.

STUFISH,
Dai Show Theatre,
Xishuangbanna,
Yunnan province,
China,
2015

A radiating faceted roof truss supports the 3D flying gates in the performance grid of the Dai Show Theatre. It forms part of the rigging system and other stage equipment, which enables performers to 'fly' from catwalk and grid areas above the performance areas, and land on – or rise from – the stage. Theatre structure design by Atelier One.

Visual Stories

It is easy to understand why many people marvel at the scale of some of the world's architectural achievements while most are blind to the complex requirements behind successful touring and theatrical performances. It is precisely because tall buildings are designed to stand alone and be admired, whereas venues are designed to play a supporting role – not to upstage the performance, but to enhance it. The process of designing a skyscraper may be very similar to that of designing an events venue, but the scope and programme are very different indeed.

After defining the brief and identifying the programmatic requirements of a venue, the creative process can begin in earnest with the production of visuals representing developed and considered concepts. These conceptual renderings, sketches, physical models and VR (virtual reality) environments most often describe a changing environment over a period of time, not a fixed and finite moment. STUFISH's visuals are more akin to animated storyboards than static, realistic CGI (computer-generated imagery) because they represent a constantly changing condition.

The design process begins by identifying a key element, often a specific term or iconic symbol that drives the creation of a narrative, though at times this narrative is driven by the show the venue will support.

The initial project narrative is represented through a series of emotive photos that begin to build an emotional experience. Many architectural practices employ the

STUFISH,
Keller Auditorium,
Portland, Oregon,
2017

The 2017 winning architectural proposal for the redevelopment of the Keller Auditorium, a 2,992-capacity venue. The proposal reconfigured the front-of-house lobby to have a greater view onto the public stage located in the heart of the Keller Fountain Park just opposite. The curving geometry of the façade also augmented the natural acoustic of the stage bowl.

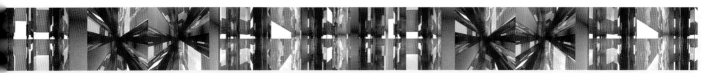

use of mood boards, as they are an efficient way to include the client in the design process and establish a clear visual path forward. Like all architects, STUFISH's proposals need to adhere to the relevant building codes and regulations, but the programme contains the added complexity of performance that permeates through the entirety of the proposal.

In its most holistic iteration the performative narrative at the centre of a show drives the language of the set, the interior design, the structure of a building, and the landscape surrounding the venue. *KÀ*, a Cirque du Soleil production in Las Vegas (2004), where the performance moved from the stage and was pushed into an immersive environment within the auditorium, is a case in point. STUFISH's design moved into the auditorium not as a decorative treatment, but as a piece of performative structure supporting critical and memorable moments in the show. Additionally, this design shattered the notion that a stage is a confined space, while redefining what a stage could be. One could make the case that *KÀ* has no stage at all but, rather, is a floating performance above a seeming abyss. With influences drawn from Japanese icons,

STUFISH,
One Za'abeel,
Dubai, United Arab Emirates,
2018

To complete a virtual scene, six square frames are rendered for the left and right eyes then stitched together. The viewing apparatus then joins these frames into a stereoscopic scene. These are often used as both a means to pitch a concept as well as a tool to develop spaces in line with design intent.

STUFISH's visuals are more akin to animated storyboards than static, realistic CGI because they represent a constantly changing condition

this concept was represented in the form of sketches, drawing on the vastness of the structure expanding over and around the audience.

Most proposals developed at STUFISH are presented via a conceptual triptych: precedent images, sketches and CG renderings. After this initial creative presentation, the work quickly evolves into animated geometric studies, parametric iterations on form-finding solutions and virtual studies examining the variety of spatial conditions that can be developed utilising a series of differing environments. Technological advances in the software used by the gaming and construction industries have been directly correlated with transformations in the entertainment industry. VR goggles, for example, are an incredibly powerful tool that not only benefits the design process but also constitutes an effective way of transporting a client, performer and/or designer into a specific moment of an event to help them better understand the proposal.

Scope and Space

Like an office block, a theatre stands as a cultural monolith within a city; but unlike an office block, when the theatre opens it breathes life and celebration to the audience inside and the wider community. One might draw a comparison with how theme park attractions are planned in such a way that events occur as part of a developing progression of the scenic environment, rather than within a solitary, confined space. The 2,000-seat live-entertainment Han Show Theatre in Wuhan, China (2014) is a good example of a building designed using a holistic approach, employing a design language that was not limited to a particular space but coursed its way from the stage at its centre out into the surrounding landscape, affecting every surface and structure in between.

STUFISH,
Han Show Theatre,
Wuhan,
China,
2014

left: The Han Show Theatre's design is influenced by the traditional Chinese paper lantern, to create an iconic Chinese symbol. The cladding, made of intersecting tubular steel rings, reinterprets the paper lantern's bamboo structure to cover the theatre's auditorium and fly tower.

opposite bottom: The theatre's auditorium is shown here with the swing-seats in an open position along with a dry thrust-stage configuration, showing the performance pool that had been concealed under the swing-seats.

Designing from the auditorium and working outwards also ensured design continuity by extending the scenic treatment and structural language beyond the venue and in so doing, expanding the impact of the performance

The theatre design was influenced by the geometry of a Chinese lantern – hence its popular name, 'the Red Lantern' – with the stage and auditorium shining at its centre. The ambition for the auditorium was to develop a space that could physically – not just figuratively – transport the audience into a different world. To achieve this goal, the basic principles behind auditorium seating, staging, lighting and scenery all needed to be reconsidered.

With the knowledge that the show would be transitioning from a dry stage into a wet stage, the configuration of the auditorium seating needed to change. The design solution to achieve this reconfiguration came in the form of lower-tier 'swing-seats' that swing open to the left and right, pivoting from a front-facing orientation into a centre-facing one. While the 1,000 lower-tier swing-seats rotate into position, the 1,000 upper-tier balcony seats slowly descend to the main level, together forming a semi-in-the-round space. This change to the seating configuration transported the audience into a new environment by revealing the 10-metre (33-foot) deep performance pool at the centre of the auditorium that had been concealed by the swing-seats.

It was imperative that STUFISH be involved from the beginning with the development and design for how this auditorium performed and transformed, due to the complexity and scope of the necessary design integration, including the need to configure all the additional front-of-house and back-of-house spaces around the auditorium. Designing from the auditorium and working outwards also ensured design continuity by extending the scenic treatment and structural language beyond the venue and in so doing, expanding the impact of the performance.

Typically, the auditorium design, inclusive of both the interior design package and dynamic theatre elements like the swing-seats, would be completed by specialist consultants. In the world of performance architecture, entertainment architects act as the mediating member for an expansive team of consultants while actively participating in the design of every element of a venue, a performance or both.

Parametric Sketching

For the National Television Awards set design at London's O2 Arena in 2020, the complexity of the proposal required a parametric program to assist in sorting through permutations of the geometry and arriving at the most favourable colour combinations. The way in which the parameters were structured not only defined the geometric grouping behind the spiralling cloud of petals but also packaged them into shop drawings and included the colour information per panel. The efficiency of these parametric programs extends from the design iteration process through to optimising the procedures for fabrication and packaging.

Tools like VR platforms, real-time render engines and parametric modelling are transforming the architectural industry, and are critical to achieving a sustainable future. These advanced visualisation and modelling platforms not only speed up the production of ideas, but liberate designers' time to think about the reasoning behind concepts and find new solutions to historical inefficiencies within the entertainment industry.

STUFISH,
National Television Awards,
O2 Arena,
London,
2020

The petals of the set catalogued by size and colour and efficiently arranged for packaging by the same parametric programs used to design the vortex of colour in which they were used.

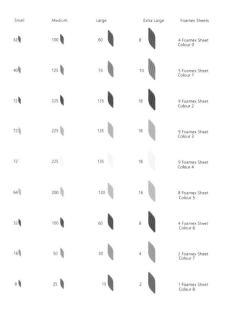

Small	Medium	Large	Extra Large	Foamex Sheets
32	100	60	8	4 Foamex Sheet Colour 0
40	125	75	10	5 Foamex Sheet Colour 1
72	225	135	18	9 Foamex Sheet Colour 2
72	225	135	18	9 Foamex Sheet Colour 3
72	225	135	18	9 Foamex Sheet Colour 4
64	200	120	16	8 Foamex Sheet Colour 5
32	100	60	8	4 Foamex Sheet Colour 6
16	50	30	4	2 Foamex Sheet Colour 7
8	25	15	2	1 Foamex Sheet Colour 8

Foamex Sheet Layout

Foamex Sheet Contents
2   15   25   8

ZUND CUT LINES

ARTWORK WITH 3MM BLEED

above: The National Television Awards 2020 set design shows the spiralling petals emanating from the centre of the stage out into the arena. They waved and rippled with colour during the show, in response to video content on the screen, through the use of LED lights and projection.

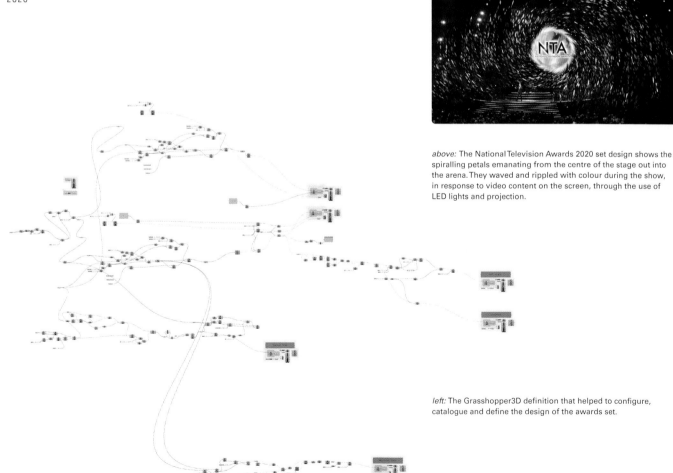

left: The Grasshopper3D definition that helped to configure, catalogue and define the design of the awards set.

Performance and Packing

While office blocks and theatres share many of the same programmatic and infrastructural conditions, the way in which they perform is substantially different. The performance of a touring stage is even more complicated, as it must function both within its own confines and within the constraints of various venues.

Moreover, it is necessary to consider the full spectrum of the requirements for producing a functional piece of entertainment architecture. For a stage set to tour efficiently, for example, the set pieces must be designed with consideration of how they will be packaged for transport.

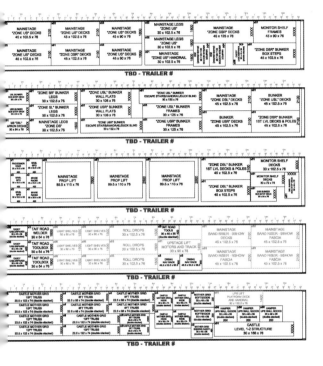

TAIT truck-packing information for Lady Gaga 'Born This Way Ball' world tour, 2012–13

For the STUFISH-designed 'Born This Way Ball' tour, TAIT TOWERS designed the stage set modules in line with truck packing studies to create the most efficient sequence of set pieces with which to tour with the least amount of trucks.

The complexity lies not only in the way the stage pieces are arranged but also in the materiality of the pieces and their cumulative weight, as these will have cost implications. To align efficiency with budget goals, a balance needs to be struck between the weight, size, and the complexity of the connections between the set's parts. This logistical dance needs to be efficient when loading out the set pieces from a venue into trucks in the quickest possible sequence. That must also be the correct sequence to allow the maximum number of a set's portions to be hoisted and assembled simultaneously once off the trucks, because touring shows are often loading into the next venue on the day of the performance. Considering how a complete stage set is packaged, how it travels, unloads and is assembled, is a choreographed performance in its own right.

The level of skill, experience, complexity, ambition and innovation required of entertainment architects is no less than that required of architects designing skyscrapers, hotels or airports. When the performances have ended, and venues have closed, the emotional fingerprints they have left with the global audiences will endure. STUFISH views its work as a continually changing event that evolves and expands as new and interesting applications come to light.

Restrictions imposed during the Covid-19 pandemic have forced designers to consider new ways in which events and venues can function, with a focus on scalability, temporality and sustainability. However, they have provided the opportunity to learn in preparation for pandemics to come. Society craves to be entertained, to be amazed, to be transported far away by story, imagination and ingenuity. STUFISH is always hard at work to keep the world awed, mesmerised and entertained, now and in the future. ᴆ

For a stage set to tour efficiently, … the set pieces must be designed with consideration of how they will be packaged for transport

Text © 2021 John Wiley & Sons Ltd. Images: pp 90–1, 93, 96 © STUFISH; pp 92, 94–5 © STUFISH, photo Raphael Oliver; p 97 © TAIT

DESIGNING PLACES FOR MAKING MEMORIES

STUFISH, Beyoncé stage set,
Coachella Valley Music and Arts Festival,
Indo, California,
2018

Rendering of the temporary one-off stage set. Simple and almost stark
in its form, it featured a pyramid flight of steps reminiscent of college
bleacher seating on which the 100 performers sat, stood and danced.
This was reflected above by an inverted pyramid structure containing
150 lights. To distinguish Beyoncé from the stage at times she was
moved through the air in a rotating, lifting boom and at other times
moved forward on a runway to a B-stage in the audience.

Robert Kronenburg

STUFISH, Willie Williams and Es Devlin Studio,
U2 'eXPERIENCE + iNNOCENCE' world tour,
2018

The 2015 'iNNOCENCE + eXPERIENCE' design utilised a barricage,
a transparent structure situated down the centre of the arena or
stadium floor through which the audience could see the band when
they moved to the satellite stage in the centre of the space, but
which also acted as a high-resolution video screen when illuminated.
The 2018 'eXPERIENCE + iNNOCENCE' STUFISH set used the same
concept with additional enhancements such as a much higher-
definition video screen, more satellite stages, and a flying catwalk
nicknamed 'The Beam'. For the first time in a touring show, audience
members could download the U2 Experience app to their smart
phones, bringing an augmented reality aspect to the show.

IMMERSIVE AUDIENCE EXPERIENCES FOR LIVE MUSIC PERFORMANCE

With his long-established interest in transient architecture, architect and academic **Robert Kronenburg** has been a longstanding friend of the STUFISH organisation. Here he probes the notion of 'reminiscence bumps', many of which are conditioned by music, concerts and shows and our experience of them. These bumps help make us into the individuals that we are and act as touchstones in our memories that traverse time.

In 2011, I was fortunate to be shown around the set of 'The Wall Live' by Mark Fisher who, with his company STUFISH, had designed this mobile show. There was a lot to see. The 90-strong crew were in the process of erecting a set 73 metres (240 feet) wide and 11 metres (36 feet) tall, spanning almost to each side of the large arena, and this was only the part the audience would see. Below the 'stage' was a vast amount of equipment that would drive the sound, vision and special effects for which this show was renowned. And afterwards, the entire thing would be taken down, packed into trucks to be re-erected at another venue 24 hours later.

The Wall, based on Pink Floyd's 1979 album, has many dramatic theatrical elements including flying (and crashing) aircraft, giant, grotesque inflatable puppets and a huge wall that is built across the stage as the show progresses before being demolished at its culmination. Coupled with stage lighting, pyrotechnics and original projected animation videos (using the constructed wall as a screen) the original 1980s version could only feasibly be mounted in four venues (31 performances in total). If the show had not already attained legendary status for its ambition, it certainly achieved it on 21 July 1990 when it was re-run, though at a much bigger scale and with worldwide publicity, in Berlin's Potsdamer Platz, shortly after the wall that divided the city was demolished pre-empting Germany's reunification. These earlier sets were designed by Fisher and his then partner engineer Jonathan Park (working as the Fisher Park Partnership), and it was only natural that when Roger Waters, Pink Floyd's bass player and the album's principal composer, decided to revive the show, he would turn to STUFISH to achieve something that had simply not been possible two decades earlier – a set that could be economically toured around the world. STUFISH would bring its experience in the development of innovative touring set technology, which made equipment lighter, more adaptable, more easily transportable and cheaper, without compromising the ambition of the performance.

Music, Memory and Place

I watched the performance that night from the mixing desk on the floor of the auditorium 100 metres (330 feet) back from the stage, and it is an experience I will never forget. A recent research study has confirmed what we all know: that music is inextricably linked with our personal autobiography, associating the significant moments in our life with what we were listening to at that time.[1] These 'reminiscence bumps' are an important element in how we construct our sense of who we are as individuals. Not surprisingly, the most important musical memories are those that are created during our formative years and so the research confirms that those made when we are 10 to 30 years old are the most resilient. This explains how the most well-known music artists (like Waters) keep packing in audiences well into their seventies. There can be no doubt that the popular young artists of today are creating their own legion of fans who will still be faithful five decades from now when they are pensioners.

STUFISH,
Pink Floyd 'The Wall Live'
world tour,
2010-13

below: 'The Wall Live' was one of the most complex rock music shows ever created, a hugely sophisticated working mechanism that combined physical and virtual elements into a cleverly orchestrated performance supporting the 12 musicians on stage. First staged in 1980 the show is based on Pink Floyd's eleventh album, a semi-autobiographical exploration of Roger Waters's experiences as a child growing up in postwar Britain and its impact on him as an adult.

bottom: Bombarded by sound, powerful visuals and surprising and impressive live-action events in the telling of a story that conveys strong messages about war trauma and mental health, the show created an immersive experience that has easily stood the test of time. Between 2010 and 2013, it was performed 219 times on four continents. In audience size and gross income, it was acknowledged as the most successful tour ever by a solo artist (only overtaken in 2019 by Ed Sheeran's '÷Tour').

STUFISH, Mark Owen and Kim Gavin,
Take That 'Greatest Hits Live' tour,
Milton Keynes, UK,
2019

opposite: Designing sets for open-air stadiums presents both problems and opportunities. The artists must be protected from inclement weather and the set must be self-supporting, but with larger audiences a greater budget can be used to create more dramatic effects. For the tour by Mark Owen, Howard Donald and Gary Barlow to mark the band's 30th anniversary the set had to work for both arenas and outdoor stadiums. The focal feature of the show was a 13-metre (43-foot) tall, 40-ton sphere that was both a video screen and a protected stage that changed form during the show.

However, although hearing the music sparks these positive emotional responses, our memories are also associated with the environment that surrounded us when we first heard it. The defining events of our lives have to happen somewhere, some *place*, and for music, that is overwhelmingly an architectural place.[2] Music happens inside rooms, basements, halls, arenas. It happens outside in city streets, urban parks, stadiums and on festival stages. The experience of music is intrinsically coupled with that of the physical environment in which it happens, and this inevitably contributes to the memories we generate during its performance. One of the most powerful musical experiences is attending a live performance by a particularly loved artist. Though they may be scripted and choreographed, each performance is a unique experience – the attributes of the venue and the character of the show shape memories of the event as much as the music the artist performed. Places of performance are where musical scenes are made 'more visible, physical, and real'.[3] A quick scan of fan forums and social media reveals that fans recall powerful reminiscences of not only the artist's performance, but every aspect of the 'going to the gig' experience: buying the ticket, the journey, meeting friends, waiting in the crowd for the show to begin, the view of the stage or battling for a good spot. Audiences who have regularly attended a particular venue or location develop a deep loyalty to 'their' club or festival, affectionately remembering its shortcomings as well as the great nights they had there. Smelly toilets, rough bouncers and muddy fields become a rite of passage that enriches their memories and deepens their affiliation to their 'tribe'.

Spectacle and Audience Connection

Though a wild night out or wet feet have their place, *spectacle* can also create powerful memories, and this dramatic addition to the experience of popular music shows began in the 1960s. Concerts in sports arenas and outdoor settings with larger audiences meant that more income could be generated per performance. The larger stage and more remote views for those at the back presented both opportunities and problems.

The possibilities of a much-expanded show 'experience' using effects and techniques transferred from musical theatre meant that the impact of live performance could be enhanced with powerful visual statements to heighten the show's emotional charge, boosting the audience's reaction and adding substantially to their sense of event.

To create these new experiences, specialist designers emerged to facilitate the growing ambitions of music artists. Mark Fisher was in the vanguard of this new design role, setting up his first company whilst still an architecture student and working with progressive rock band Pink Floyd from 1977. The practice he formed, that became STUFISH, is almost certainly the most experienced group of designers working in this field today. Describing themselves as entertainment architects, they are an interdisciplinary team that meld innovative creativity with technical know-how. Their ambition is to create memorable experiences for audiences, ironing out the logistical and technical problems that inevitably get in the way when you are trying to do something that has not been seen anywhere before. Their main area of work is in creating and realising stage experiences, both touring and for

STUFISH,
Mylène Farmer 'Timeless' tour,
Paris,
2013

The French singer's tour to support her sixth studio album featured a dramatic and highly memorable opening sequence using a giant LED screen harmonised with a mobile physical set that was modelled on the real Large Hadron Collider, enhanced into an audio-visual spectacle. Spectacular shows such as this create long-lasting impressions on their audiences and STUFISH note that this opening is something that new clients frequently reference when discussing what their own unique design might become.

important one-off events, but they are also engaged in creating permanent theatre setups that excel in flexibility and adaptability to new types of immersive audience experience. A constant factor is that innovation is a key demand from their clients, and consequently their ambitions often go beyond 'reality' to make enhanced versions of lifetime experience in which spectacle and fantasy are essential.

Always Something *New*

Mobile stages are designed for differentiation; the artists who commission them demand that they be unique and specific to their image and brand. It is crucial to them that the collective audience memory of their particular show cannot be associated with anyone else's music. This constant search for novelty and innovation has led to the development of ingenious skills and techniques by designers like STUFISH and the specialist contractors they collaborate with. Most shows utilise highly adaptable components that can be rearranged in numerous ways like a highly sophisticated construction toy, enabling a completely new, highly impressive appearance to emerge from a set of standardised parts.

Amongst the many artists that STUFISH has a long-term relationship with is the Irish rock group U2. Fisher first worked with the band and their creative director Willie Williams on the first of their more elaborately staged concert tours: 'ZOOTV' in 1992–3. The band's touring sets have since then been marked by their strong ambition to connect with every member of the audience, overcoming the limitations that large arena and stadium shows present in this regard. Each set design has involved new technical innovations in order to achieve this goal. 1997's 'PopMart' introduced the largest LED-powered video screen ever made to that date, bringing a new standard of connection with the musicians' stage performance. In 2009 the band began their '360°' tour, its title describing the objective of the unique stage set that had been created, a giant four-legged steel structure nicknamed 'The Claw' that sat at the centre of the open-air stadiums in which they performed. The band's most recent world tours 'iNNOCENCE + eXPERIENCE' (2015), 'eXPERIENCE + iNNOCENCE' (2018) and 'The Joshua Tree' (2017 and 2019) revisited and upgraded how video screens work, changing their location and character and using augmented reality to enhance further their connection with the audience whilst still providing a uniquely recognisable spectacle associated only with U2.

More Than Entertainment

Touring and festival stages are investments on which a return is planned for and expected. Audiences willingly pay to see their favourite artists and without this financial exchange the spectacle would not take place. However, live music is a cultural activity too and the audiences are not passive consumers but active participants with a personal engagement in this popular contemporary art form that reflects as well as informs society. Fans believe it is an expression of who they are, embracing social expectations and politics as well as

STUFISH,
U2 'The Joshua Tree' world tours,
2017 and 2019

Based on imagery from U2's eponymous 1987 album and tour, this mobile set design aimed to immerse the audience in visuals by suspending the amplification equipment out of the line of sight. A huge 61 × 14 metre (200 × 46 foot) screen that featured the highest resolution (7.6K) ever used in a touring show, employed imagery that connected with both the history of the band and the vast desert landscape of the Joshua Tree National Park to create a hyper-real experience for the audience.

STUFISH,
The Queen's Diamond Jubilee
Concert temporary stage,
London,
2012

This temporary stage was set up on The Mall in front of Buckingham Palace for a celebration event for Queen Elizabeth II's diamond jubilee. With an on-site audience of 10,000, up to 500,000 watched on giant screens set up nearby, and the concert was also screened to 15 million live on the BBC. Centred on the historic Queen Victoria Memorial, the structure utilised standardised components in a cantilevered roof that reflected the urban landscape surrounding the memorial and the temporary stands set up for the audience, whilst allowing the Palace to form a unique backdrop for the show.

Most shows utilise highly adaptable components that can be rearranged in numerous ways like a highly sophisticated construction toy

fashion, art and commerce. The *Wall* concert that took place in Berlin in 1990 was a powerful political message, not only to the 400,000 or so who attended it, but to audiences in the 52 countries to which it was televised live. A more recent culturally and politically important show was Beyoncé's performance at the Coachella Valley Music and Arts Festival near Los Angeles in 2018.

The show was designed to be a thematic celebration of the crucial importance of African American universities and colleges and has been described as 'resplendent and genuinely paradigm-shifting'[4] and 'rich with history, potently political and visually grand'.[5] This headline show was both a live and a virtual experience as Coachella has been an innovator in global streaming of live performances. A Netflix documentary (*Homecoming,* 2019) in which Beyoncé talks passionately about the many social and political aspects that inspired its creation reinforced its international impact.

Music is a social activity, centred around architecturally designed spaces and places that energise and enliven city life, stimulating other supporting enterprises and businesses. Music scenes, whether in a small club or a gigantic festival stage, are places where diverse groups of people gather to make moments that they will remember and reflect on for the rest of their lives. Large shows that use sophisticated, ambitious mobile stage sets have encouraged the creation of a new architectural building type, the large indoor urban arena, with 16 built in the UK alone, most of these in the last 20 years. Entertainment architects like STUFISH deliver two unique qualities to these large-scale live music experiences, one that has always been there and one that is new with this phenomenon. The first quality is something that is easily accessible in a small club but notoriously difficult in a 20,000-seat arena: to enable and encourage audiences to be a real part of the show by striving hard for an immersive experience in which the individual can engage. The second quality is something that can only be economically achieved with this size of audience (and consequent budget): to present an event which is simultaneously real and a fantasy, whether it is a direct connection with your fabulously famous (and in normal circumstances remote) hero, or an audio-visual spectacle that leaves your heart pounding. To create amazing things happening right in front of your eyes that you will never, ever forget – that is entertainment architecture. ⌂

Notes
1. See Kelly Jakubowski *et al*, 'A Cross-Sectional Study of Reminiscence Bumps for Music-Related Memories in Adulthood', *Music & Science*, 3 (13), 2020: https://journals.sagepub.com/doi/pdf/10.1177/2059204320965058.
2. See Robert Kronenburg, *This Must Be The Place: An Architectural History of Popular Music Performance Venues,* Bloomsbury (New York), 2019.
3. Sarah Cohen, 'Scenes', in Bruce Horner and Thomas Swiss (eds), *Key Terms in Popular Music Culture*, Blackwell (Oxford), 1999, pp 239–50.
4. Jake Nevins, 'Homecoming Review – Beyoncé Documentary is a Triumphant Celebration', *The Guardian,* 18 April 2019: www.theguardian.com/film/2019/apr/18/homecoming-beyonce-review-documentary-is-a-triumphant-celebration.
5. Jon Caramanica, 'Review: Beyoncé Is Bigger Than Coachella', *The New York Times,* 15 April 2018: www.nytimes.com/2018/04/15/arts/music/beyonce-coachella-review.html.

FROM NICE IDEAS TO THEIR MORTAL REMAINS

PINK FLOYD AT THE V&A

Victoria Broackes

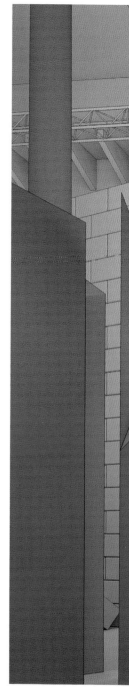

STUFISH,
Concept sketch
for 'Pink Floyd:
Their Mortal
Remains' exhibition,
Victoria and
Albert Museum,
London,
May–October 2017

left: Initial concept sketch during the planning of the exhibition inspired by artwork for the *Momentary Lapse of Reason* studio album (released 1987). It was never realised on this scale, except for the idea of bed units that one could listen to; these were used in different versions of the exhibition.

Currently Director of the London Design Biennale, **Victoria Broackes** was previously Senior Curator for the Department of Theatre and Performance at London's Victoria and Albert Museum, where she was instrumental in assembling some of the museum's blockbuster music exhibitions. One of the most visited and iconic was 2017's 'Pink Floyd: Their Mortal Remains'. Here she tells its story.

Picturing a museum exhibition may bring to mind images of people milling about, quietly considering art hung on white walls in clean frames or walking slowly around a plinth peering at an object held inside a glass box. For London's Victoria and Albert Museum (V&A), music exhibitions such as 'David Bowie is ...' (2013–18) and 'You Say You Want a Revolution? Records and Rebels 1966–1970' (2016–17) demanded an experience that was a stark departure from, even a repudiation of, the traditional way of viewing a show. These exhibitions functioned almost as a hybrid performance/exhibition – distilling and evoking the experience one gets from music and concerts and placing it alongside objects, costumes and artefacts illustrating the cultural impact of the subject. 'Pink Floyd: Their Mortal Remains', which opened at the V&A in May 2017, perfectly realised this approach.

'Pink Floyd: Their Mortal Remains' took pristine white-light exhibitions through a prism of collaboration to refract a multicoloured, multisensory experience to tell the story of Pink Floyd's sound and design, and capture the experience of their performances and their life journey. Developing music-based exhibitions requires much working across disciplines, and while it is obvious to assume the importance of 2D graphic, exhibition and sound designers, with Pink Floyd as the subject, the architecture was the crucial element that integrated the project.

For this exhibition, STUFISH was uniquely positioned to design and realise immersive experiences for the audience, as its history with the band goes back to the 1970s. Together they helped drive forward the subsequent revolution in stadium rock tours, performance architecture and exhibition design.

Revolutionary Theatre and Inflatable Flying Pigs

Pink Floyd, one of the first British psychedelic rock groups, was co-founded in 1965 by Syd Barrett, Roger Waters, Richard Wright and Nick Mason, joined by David Gilmour in 1967. Waters took on the role of frontman and primary songwriter after Barrett's departure in 1968, and he himself left in 1985.

The revolutionary and theatrical way Pink Floyd presented their music was already renowned in London's underground music scene before they began working with Mark Fisher, who later went on to found STUFISH, and the engineer Jonathan Park with whom Fisher set up the Fisher Park Partnership in 1984. Pink Floyd never stopped thinking up new ways to 'offer a well-presented theatre show' as Syd Barrett explained in 1967.[1] For example, a Pink Floyd performance in May 1967 at the newly opened Queen Elizabeth Hall on London's South Bank featured a light show and the Azimuth Co-ordinator quadrophonic sound system, recorded birdsong, staged log chopping, the distribution of daffodils to the audience and a bubble machine (the effects of which resulted in their first performance at the Hall also being their last).

STUFISH and Aubrey Powell,
'The Wall' model, 'Pink Floyd:
Their Mortal Remains' exhibition,
Victoria and Albert Museum,
London,
May–October 2017

One section of the exhibition allowed visitors a close-up view of the reconstructed Wall and several of the surreal inflatable puppets, as well as the model plane that 'crashed' into the stage, that were used during the live tour.

STUFISH and Aubrey Powell,
Re-creation of motel room from
Pink Floyd 'The Wall' tour,
'Pink Floyd: Their Mortal
Remains' exhibition,
Victoria and Albert Museum,
London,
May-October 2017

This exhibit in one of the rooms devoted to
Pink Floyd's individual live shows recreated an
iconic visual from the band's 'The Wall' tour
(1982) in which a man in the throes of a mental
breakdown sits in a motel room watching the
epic war film *The Dam Busters* (1955) on TV.

By the early 1970s, Pink Floyd were beginning to experiment with what would become one of their trademarks – inflatables in live performance. On 15 May 1971, they headlined the Crystal Palace Garden Party rock concert at London's Crystal Palace Bowl, and while they played material from the album *Atom Heart Mother* (1970), a huge inflatable octopus, created by artists Jeffrey Shaw and Theo Botschuijver of Eventstructure Research Group, emerged from the depths of the lake surrounded by orange mist. Previously, Shaw had impressed the members of the band when they saw his performative art installation *Pneutube* in 1969, which exposed them to pneumatics in entertainment. This new interest in pneumatics matched developments in architectural theory about air, art and light structures. Concurrently, Fisher, an architecture student at London's Architectural Association (AA) between 1965 and 1971, was developing his own practice in pneumatics and temporary structures.

Fisher studied under Peter Cook of Archigram, an avant-garde architectural collective founded at the AA whose mostly unrealised conceptual designs challenged the perceived need for architecture to be static, instead championing technologically driven, lightweight, mobile environments capable of enhancing human interaction, informed by influences from the wider context of art, architecture, technology and philosophy.[2] Like others at the AA, including engineer and soon-to-be collaborator Jonathan Park, Fisher was interested in the work of the American inventor Richard Buckminster Fuller, developer of the geodesic dome, and also that of the German architect-engineer Frei Otto, whose pioneering experiments with lightweight structures, tensile fabrics and adaptable architecture were often inspired by natural phenomena.

Flexible Architecture – A Moveable Feast

Like their predecessors in Archigram, Mark Fisher, Jonathan Park and their collaborators were working at the intersection of advanced technology and barely imaginable concepts. However, they realised that rock and roll provided the ideal practical and possibly the only real-world application for these big ideas and flexible, portable environments. Propelled by the creative ambitions of bands and their designers, innovations in major staging components in the 1970s – rigging, trucking and automatic ticketing, as well as sound and video technology – changed the face of the rock-and-roll tour forever. These ideas found traction with Pink Floyd's concepts and innovative approach to staging, and in Park and Fisher the band were to find expert and daring collaborators who were a perfect match to help them create and realise their ambitious visions.

In 1976, the production designer Andrew Sanders approached Fisher to collaborate on inflatable sculptures for the 'Animals / In the Flesh' tour (*Animals* album released 1977) in conjunction with Park, who had been commissioned to engineer a mechanical motorised system which would allow the structures to 'fly'. As well as the emblematic inflatable pig – a version of which was dragged out of retirement and flown above the V&A on Press launch day – Fisher and Sanders drew on the album's dystopian themes of a flawed capitalist society. They designed a larger-than-life inflatable family (a businessman and housewife and their 2.5 porky children), orbited by the accoutrements of their 'average' household (a fridge full to bursting, a television and a hot-pink Cadillac).

'Animals / In the Flesh' brought about a significant development to the generic roof structure of rock architecture that had been a staple of the stadium show since the 1969 Woodstock music festival in Bethel,

STUFISH and Aubrey Powell,
Delicate Sound of Thunder diorama,
'Pink Floyd: Their Mortal Remains' exhibition,
Victoria and Albert Museum,
London,
May–October 2017

Delicate Sound of Thunder (1988) was Pink Floyd's first live album. The album cover included an image of a man in a suit covered with light bulbs. This diorama in the exhibition reproduces the one photographed for the cover of the album's 2017 remastered edition.

New York. Inspired by Frei Otto and Günter Behnisch's lightweight membrane tented roof structure for the 1972 Munich Olympics and Otto's 'Large Umbrellas' at Cologne's Federal Garden Exhibition in 1971, the band worked with Otto and engineer Ted Happold of Buro Happold to create a stage set which was fully integrated with the wider space. They commissioned collapsible umbrellas which provided rain cover for the stage in what Fisher described as 'quite a subtle approach to the issue of presenting a show in a stadium because it showed an awareness of the existence of the stadium and did not choose to ignore its adjacent architecture'.[3]

For the live world tour of *The Wall* in 1980 (album released 1979), Fisher and Park were approached to find and realise a spectacular but achievable solution to stage the show, which was in essence an intricate,

moving, mobile theatrical musical featuring characters, a storyline, stage-effects, puppetry, sleight-of-hand, a decoy band, projected films and an animated, sculptural stage set that evolved throughout the show as, brick by brick, the wall was built between the band and audience.

Not only was 'The Wall' innovative in terms of concept and narrative, but the stage set itself broke new ground in terms of the logistics of rock touring to arena venues. As Fisher explained: 'It was a piece of rock and roll touring theatre which was engaging with the [indoor] arena in the same way as I was interested in trying to deal with the stadium – it was actually taking the show and the arena and saying these things together are the experience of the evening – not just sitting looking at a proscenium stage.'[4]

The eponymous tour that followed the release of the album *The Division Bell* in 1994 was Fisher's first collaboration with the post-Waters-era Pink Floyd and was, at the time, the highest-grossing rock tour ever. This was also the year he dissolved the Fisher Park Partnership and established Mark Fisher Studios, which would later become STUFISH. By that time the logistics of stage-show touring had developed significantly and rock shows were able to move more efficiently from venue to venue. Working with construction partners from the staging industry, Fisher sought to modify existing truss components to create a modular and, crucially, a replicable solution for the staging.

STUFISH and Setsquare Creative,
Building 'The Wall' for the 'Pink Floyd:
Their Mortal Remains' exhibition,
Victoria and Albert Museum,
London,
May–October 2017

The 7.5-metre (25-foot) model of 'The Wall' for the V&A exhibition being built at Setsquare Creative's studios. The original 12-metre (40-foot) wall was built of cardboard bricks for Pink Floyd's 'The Wall' world tour (1980–81). The concept came from the band's Roger Waters, whose idea it was to begin building a wall between the band and the audience during the course of each show until, at the end, they could no longer see each other.

Bringing Retrospection to Life

V&A Theatre & Performance curators first approached
Fisher at STUFISH in 2008 and together worked
through proposals for a range of possible exhibitions
at the V&A. Sadly, it was only several years after
Mark's passing in 2013 that the definitive opportunity
for a V&A/STUFISH show presented itself. He would
probably have been amused to see two giant *Division
Bell* heads, wheeled through the V&A with great care,
taking their place in the exhibition.

The design of the 'Pink Floyd: Their Mortal Remains'
exhibition sought to capture the multi-stranded
relationship between Fisher and Park, STUFISH, the
band, and the band's graphic designers Hipgnosis,
co-founded by Storm Thorgerson and Aubrey Powell
– who was also the creative director for the exhibition
(see his article on pp 38–45 of this issue). The results
of these collaborations not only created a spectacular
theatrical environment in the temporary space of the
exhibition but one that felt almost spiritually connected
to its subject.

An exhibition allows the audience to move at
their own pace and focus on areas which most
resonate with their own personal interests, stories
and memories. Exhibitions are an embodiment of our
hyperlinked world – engaging and presenting multiple
ideas, juxtapositions, sounds and visuals, often
simultaneously and more effectively than the linear
formats of a film, a play or a book.

In 'Pink Floyd: Their Mortal Remains' the music
was treated either as an object or as an integral part
of the narrative throughout. In the area dedicated to
sonic experimentation, a display of instruments and
synthesisers was enlivened by giving the public the
opportunity to use a mixing desk to remix the track
'Money'. Sometimes immersion allowed visitors the
space to engage with the music without being told
what to feel. A dark room was dedicated to *The Dark
Side of the Moon* (released 1973) which simply had
the album playing in its entirety and a hologram of a
spinning prism on display, echoing the design of the
album cover. Performance areas with louder sound
were created to evoke the communal feeling of live
music. This was manifest in the 'Pink Floyd Live' zone
at the end of the exhibition.

The architecture section, shown within the immense
stage-set towers of the Battersea Power Station, was
an opportunity to show the Pink Floyd set designs
in the context of objects from the V&A architectural
collections. Aspirational concepts including the Fun
Palace (1961) conceived by architect Cedric Price in
collaboration with avant-garde theatre practitioner Joan
Littlewood, and the Instant City designed by Archigram
(1968–70), illustrated how theory, academia, architects,
music, touring architecture and, now, museum
exhibitions are linked.

Time for Some Nice Ideas

Developments in VR (virtual reality), AR (augmented
reality), gaming technology and motion capture are

STUFISH and Aubrey Powell,
Rabbit-hole tunnel,
'Pink Floyd: Their Mortal Remains' exhibition,
Victoria and Albert Museum,
London,
May–October 2017

London's 1960s underground psychedelic scene was evoked in the
exhibition via this Bridget Riley-esque rabbit-hole tunnel through
which visitors had to pass. Pink Floyd developed an early reputation
for shows incorporating inventive light projections which created a
sonic experience, matching and augmenting the kind of psychedelic
environment they performed in; their audiences would spend hours
bathed in a psyche-scape of sounds and colour.

STUFISH and Aubrey Powell,
Replica of Pink Floyd's Bedford van,
'Pink Floyd: Their Mortal
Remains' exhibition,
Victoria and Albert Museum,
London,
May–October 2017

Visitors accessed the exhibition via an oversized replica of Pink Floyd's famous Bedford van – here seen under construction. The beaten-up old touring vehicle, made instantly recognisable by a customised paint job, was used to ferry the group and their equipment between gigs in the mid-1960s, when they were just starting out.

having a big impact on entertainment and in creating personally tailored journeys for future museum displays. They have allowed performances to 'tour' without the performers themselves, an especially significant shift during the Covid-19 pandemic. Following the mass media pivot towards streaming, predictions of the end of large-scale touring structures have been debated in the media. However, there are indications that people are very much looking forward to re-engaging in live shared experiences. It might be the time for another new leap forward – the next generation is making a huge impact on shared culture by speaking out against climate change and racial injustice; it is hard to imagine that these concerns will not impact entertainment architecture. The environmental costs of touring will likely be at the forefront of future debates within the music industry, entertainment sector and in museums.

Faced with an unknown future it is tempting to fall back on the familiar. Yet the willingness to see what permutations are possible, to use things in different ways and times than originally intended, is the essence of unorthodox, collaborative creativity. The spirit of Mark Fisher's thinking is in the DNA of STUFISH's work; times of change are an opportunity for innovation – time for some Nice Ideas.[5] ⌀

Notes

1. Alan Walsh, 'Hits? The Floyd Couldn't Care Less', interview in *Melody Maker*, 9 December 1967: www.pink-floyd.org/artint/mmdec67.htm.
2. For more information, see the Archigram Archival Project: http://archigram.westminster.ac.uk/.
3. Mark Fisher, 'Tribe Style', Architecture Association lecture, 23 May 2000, www.aaschool.ac.uk/publicprogramme/whatson/tribe-style.
4. *Ibid*.
5. Thanks are due to many people for helping to make this article possible, particularly my V&A colleague Samantha Wassmer.

The music was treated either as an object or as an integral part of the narrative throughout

TECHNOLOGY AND AUDIENCE AS CURATOR

Willie Williams and Mark Fisher,
U2 'PopMart' world tour,
Las Vegas, Nevada,
1997

Following the visual breakthrough of the 'ZooTV' tour, Fisher and Williams proposed to U2 the idea of creating a low-resolution LED video screen on an open structure, large enough to fill the end of a stadium. Unique at the time, this approach remains the industry standard for large-format touring video screens. The aesthetic is borrowed from mid-century architecture and pop culture, combining the spectacular with the absurd.

IN CONVERSATION WITH PRODUCTION DESIGNER WILLIE WILLIAMS

STUFISH partner **Ric Lipson** talks to **Willie Williams**, who has been a key show director, stage and lighting designer and creative visionary of live entertainment for 40 years. Originally collaborating with STUFISH founder Mark Fisher (then of Fisher Park Partnership) beginning in 1992, the relationship between Williams and the STUFISH studio has created a plethora of innovative stage designs. Here they look forward to see how future audiences might experience such work and how designers need to react to the technological changes that are coming.

When Willie Williams was interviewed about the future of entertainment design in 2007, he predicted that the 'future will be a relentless tsunami of LED-encrusted mediocrity, and no one will care'.[1] Since then, he has conceded that the intervening period has produced 'its wonders of entertainment architecture' and that perhaps he was 'taking an overly dim view of both creators and consumers but, in fairness, those moments of originality have been rare'.

According to Williams, a common feeling in the world of show design is that great advances in technology have also brought 'a disappointment at the homogenisation of the way shows were starting to look'. The advent of moving lights during the 1980s had produced a similar result: 'It's not surprising that the introduction of a new design technology brings profound change, but in both cases, it hasn't always been beneficial to the creative process.'

Architects constantly wrestle with the question of whether the design happens in the designer's mind, or through the manipulation of software originally created for aviation and other industries. Despite this ambiguity, within the world of architecture the arrival of computer-aided design in the 1980s opened up 'entirely new avenues of creativity, and with that came a great diversity'. Structures could now be built that would have been impossible using a pen-on-paper approach. Future Systems, Frank Gehry, Zaha Hadid and countless others mastered the new processes to create radically new and entirely individual work that is instantly recognisable, despite using an essentially similar range of tools.

In live entertainment, however, it seems the polar opposite has happened. Williams believes that 'far from spawning diversity and originality, for the most part, if you take the performer out of the picture, show environments have often become almost entirely interchangeable'. The act of 'design' is frequently reduced to selecting options from built-in menus. This is not just specific to off-the-shelf video, lighting and staging products; lighting and video control and content servers are manufactured to incorporate an arsenal of pre-made effects: 'If so much of how an environment looks now depends on the innate capabilities of the equipment, it raises the question of where the act of creation really lies. Arguably, what we're seeing is largely the product of the equipment manufacturers, who clearly have a different agenda than those wishing to create original shows.'

RESISTING CLICHÉS TO ADVANCE THE FORM
As creative collaborators, challenging these restrictions has been a founding principal of STUFISH and Williams's work, and we are fortunate to have found clients and collaborators who feel as passionately about this as we do. Williams explains: 'Even within my own body of work I have tried to resist falling into clichés by repeating a winning formula too often.' Some of the earliest large-scale multimedia touring stadium shows designed by Fisher and Williams were U2's 'ZooTV'

and 'PopMart', from 1992 to 1998, which are widely acknowledged as having completely transformed concert visuals, setting the template for what followed 'However, in the context of U2, I was keen not to repea the idea indefinitely. Mark Fisher and I spent several years contemplating what could follow; what could compete with the visual saturation brought by large-format video in a live context.'

U2 and Willie Williams invited Fisher Park to reinvent the design of the indoor 'ZooTV' show for stadiums, incorporating the visual language of the television outside broadcast.

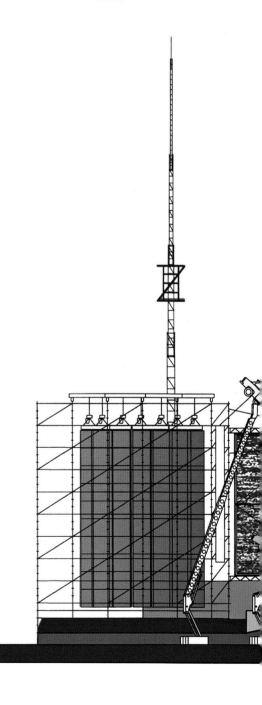

Willie Williams,
R.E.M. 'Up' tour,
Mountainview,
California,
1999

One hundred rope light motifs
were fabricated in China,
combining the aesthetic of
Chinese festival decorations
with Western clip-art images.

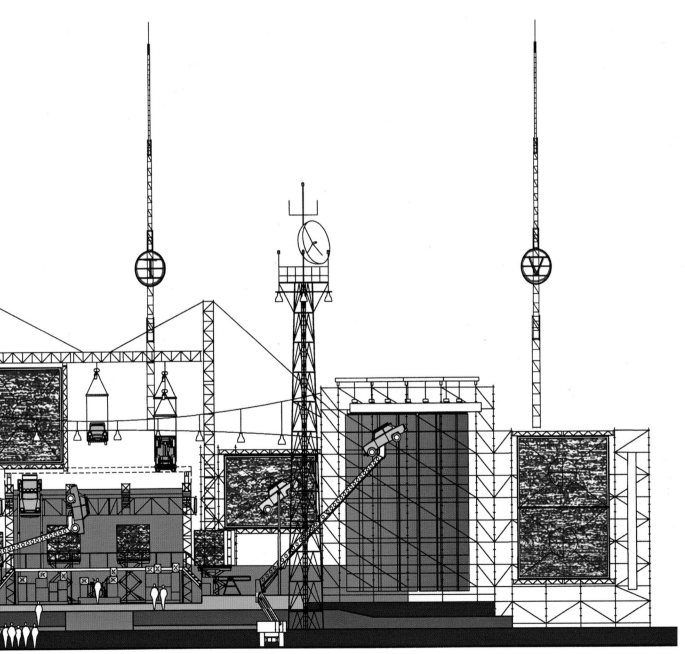

Their response was the design for the U2 '360°' world tour (2009–11), which replaced the centrality of the video image with a more sculptural thought: 'In whichever stadium this played, the expansive structure drew the entire stadium into being part of the design architecture of the show.' In 2013, STUFISH and Williams developed this approach for the Robbie Williams 'Take the Crown' tour, using 3D-scanned heads of the artist to create large kinetic sculptural floats, together with the first 3D video screen backdrop as a way of really questioning the nature and potential uses of a video screen.

The recent advent of brighter, more lightweight, see-through and tourable screens has allowed us to engage with video content on our own terms to challenge the existing forms. Williams says: 'This was done with U2 during their most recent touring period (2015–19) either by expanding and simplifying the idea of the screen to create a vast, immersive experience ['The Joshua Tree' world tours, 2017 and 2019] or by merging performers, staging, imagery and audience into a single narrative canvas ['iNNOCENCE + eXPERIENCE' tour, 2015, and 'eXPERIENCE + iNNOCENCE' tour, 2018].'

Willie Williams, STUFISH
and Es Devlin Studio,
U2 'iNNOCENCE + eXPERIENCE' world tour,
Berlin,
2015

The 'barricage' was a bespoke hybrid object
combining staging, lighting and video. It allowed
the merging of performers and visual imagery
in an in-the-round performance environment.

Willie Williams
and STUFISH,
U2 '360°' world tour,
Barcelona,
2009

Responding to a desire to step back
from a video-led production design,
Williams and Fisher proposed an
in-the-round stage, the sheer scale of
which would create intimacy within
each stadium. Weighing 200 tonnes
and carrying a further 250-tonne load,
the legs of the colossal structure
tapered to just one metre at their
narrowest point.

Experimentation at this scale requires a highly
willing and engaged client, so it is easy to identify show
designs that have been artist-led. Williams believes that
'ultimately it has to be the performer's show, but many
musicians and performers lack design experience, so
the collaborative team becomes key to a successful
process. I often liken my work to making somebody
else's wedding dress; it has to work for the wearer rather
than the designer, but we do our best to make them look
as magnificent as possible.'

He has an interesting take on our role as designers
working with these high-profile artists in driving the
whole industry: 'It might be compared to the difference
between an architect creating important architecture
versus merely designing functional housing. In the
end, both are necessary, but it would be nice to think
that some of the creative aspirations of the leaders
contribute to lifting the whole form.'

FORM FOLLOWS CONTENT

As artists move towards more narrative-driven shows,
and new technologies develop to bring these stories to
life in both the physical and digitally enhanced worlds,
boundaries are being pushed in different areas. The
way entertainment is now consumed also plays a part
in this dynamic. Williams says: 'With the landscape
of entertainment consumption having changed so
fundamentally, it would be foolish to imagine that this
wouldn't profoundly affect the live-show experience, for
performer and audience alike.'

He thinks one of these profound changes is taking
place inside the performers' process. Social media now
leads the aesthetic presence of any music artist, rather
than the promo videos, MTV, album covers, etc central
to previous generations of performers: 'If the creative
process begins with social media, inevitably the key
creative people around an artist are likely to be from
this world.' Consequently, when it comes to creating
a live show, the creative stance is more likely to come
from this viewpoint, rather than from set designers and
architects who may have traditionally held these key
roles: 'In a sense, the design process becomes much
more content-led, rather than environment-led.'

A new visual language of personality-based social
media captures and promotes artists' digital presence
almost entirely in the form of the close-up. Williams
explains that 'this has been a natural fit for concert
video screens, perhaps at the expense of more creative
ideas. As a result, the role of physical staging seems to
be less important. If the apparatus delivers the content,
many performers appear to feel that the design goal has
been achieved. Perhaps designers have a new role now,
or at least a new set of parameters to accept.'

Audience use of mobile phones is often cited as
detrimental to the live entertainment experience. For
a performer, there can be a catastrophic loss of focus
when audience members are dividing their attention
between the event and their phone, but from the
audience's point of view, their mobile is not necessarily
an intrusion. 'The next wave might say that phones

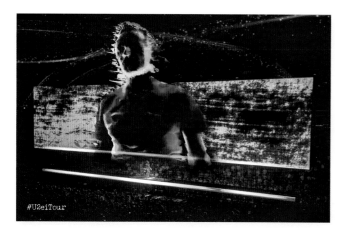

Willie Williams, STUFISH and Es Devlin Studio,
'eXPERIENCE + iNNOCENCE' world tour,
Tulsa, Oklahoma,
2018

During the opening number of the show, a bespoke app created by Treatment Studio allowed audience members to view a giant, ephemeral avatar of U2's Bono, apparently lip-syncing with the live vocal.

MOBILE-PHONE USE BRINGS ANOTHER CHANGE: THE AUDIENCE, AND SOMETIMES THE ARTIST, SHARE PARTS OR EVEN ALL OF THE SHOW ONLINE

A 40-minute pre-show augmented-reality sequence was designed to allow viewers to become familiar with the technique, without the need for written instructions.

and wearables may well become vital or even central to the concert experience', says Williams. For the U2 'eXPERIENCE + iNNOCENCE' tour in 2018 we explored an augmented-reality app where people could hold up their phone and see an extended digital layer applied to the physical performance.

However, it was interesting to witness an audience responding to the opening act of U2's 'The Joshua Tree' show in 2017; the first 20 minutes were conducted in the stadium under simple lighting with no video reinforcement at all, the band huddled on a small satellite stage, surrounded by the crowd. Williams recounts that 'for viewers beyond the first few rows there was very little to look at, never mind attempt to photograph. The sound, of course, was enormous, and with the audience singing pulled the entire place into sharp focus. It was amusing to see how remarkably quickly the sea of cell-phone lights diminished as focus was drawn entirely to the source of the sound.'

This was a reminder that the sense of connection that comes from being at a live show used to be a very direct relationship between performer and viewer; personal, location-specific and in real time. But, 'perhaps we might have to accept that for the coming generation, a live event provides a more abstract, broader connection between the participant and their wider community, over a longer period of time'.

AUDIENCE AS CURATOR

Mobile-phone use brings another change: the audience, and sometimes the artist, share parts or even all of the show online. Williams discusses a show he designed for George Michael in 2006: 'We rehearsed the show in Barcelona, with all the attendant highs and lows the rehearsal process brings. The result was very positive and by the end George was delighted with what we had made. However, the morning after opening night, he came into the venue, still very positive, but with lots of notes about the show. These he had put together entirely from watching clips of it on the then-nascent YouTube.'

This was a first for Williams, but he realised immediately that this was the future: 'A few years later, my brief tenure with Lady Gaga made it abundantly clear that the way a show presents on social media will define how it is remembered – and indeed if it is remembered at all.' Much as this thought appalls his perfectionist instincts, he has also come to see that there is a potentially positive aspect to the arrangement.

Although this extended view is not equivalent to the live experience, it nonetheless allows distant fans to engage in the work. However, it is important to remember that 'the essence of live performance is a real-time, location-specific relationship between humans. It is about creating an environment where a magical energy-exchange can take place between performer and viewer, which, at its very best, can forge a lasting emotional connection of a kind rarely experienced elsewhere in life. It sounds impossibly grand, but I've seen it often enough to appreciate that

Willie Williams,
George Michael '25 Live' tour,
Barcelona,
2006

For George Michael's return to live performance
after a 15-year hiatus, Williams's production and
video design merged stage, backdrop and audience
thrust into a single, continuous video surface.

he memories we create really can become emotional milestones in people's lives.'

The explorations in entertainment design during the Covid-19 pandemic have demonstrated this. Whereas it has been interesting to witness the new creative forms being developed, Williams believes that the lockdowns will demonstrate that there is no truly satisfying substitute for the live experience: 'The "virtual show" is more likely to become established as a new form in its own right than to continue to attempt to mimic the real thing. In time I'm sure there will be demand for both, which would be a good longer-term result for the entertainment industry.'

The downside of the genuinely humbling privilege of creating and sharing these memory-making moments is their evanescence, but Williams has long made peace with the fact that he has spent his life creating work of a temporary and highly ephemeral nature: 'Sure, there may be the artefacts, the exhibitions, the photographs, but really these capture and celebrate everything other than the actual experience.' He recounts a wonderful quote by avant-garde dancer and choreographer Merce Cunningham that addresses this frustrating impermanence: 'You have to love dancing to stick to it. It gives nothing back, no manuscripts to store away, no paintings to show on walls and maybe hang in museums, no poems to be printed and sold, nothing but that single fleeting moment when you feel alive.'[2]

Williams has come to embrace the notion that there is something interesting and worthwhile about the YouTube phenomenon: 'For the new generation of live entertainment consumers – the K-pop show, the EDM festival, the club night out – each audience member is curating their own experience of your work.' As the once-ephemeral memory of a show is now lived and curated by the audience, he believes that this new kind of connection might be one we should strive to enhance, and that perhaps the permanent act of creation now lies with each of them, all of them together, rather than with the designer or the equipment manufacturer. ⏁

This article is based on an interview with Willie Williams in London in February 2021.

Notes
1. Marian Sandberg , 'Q+A: Willie Williams', Live Design online, 1 September 2007: www.livedesignonline.com/concerts/q-a-willie-williams.
2. Merce Cunningham, *Changes: Notes on Choreography* [1968], The Song Cave/Merce Cunningham Trust (New York), 2019, p 92.

Ray Winkler

'To Thrill You, I'll Use Any Device'

An Interview with Queen founder members Brian May and Roger Taylor

STUFISH,
Queen + Adam Lambert 'Rhapsody' world tour,
Tacoma, Washington,
July 2019

'Guitar solo': a key moment in the show when Brian May rises into the sky on top of an asteroid surrounded by kinetic, illuminated planets and immersed in an environment of stars and laser beams.

What about the bands that grace STUFISH stages – the clients of entertainment architecture? In an intimate and exclusive interview with Queen founder members **Brian May and Roger Taylor**, Guest-Editor of this △ issue and STUFISH Design Director **Ray Winkler** explores their perspectives on gigging, past and present. Much has changed over the course of the rock group's more than 50-year history, from the theatrical nature of performances to the technology, sound and visuals. They offer their thoughts on it all.

Queen's unique mix of hard rock, musical theatre and opera has become so iconic that it is hard to remember that when they began playing together, in the early 1970s, audience participation at concerts was minimal. As Brian May says: 'We come from a time and place where it wasn't very cool to have a production at all, when rock concerts were mostly done in quite dim lighting, with not the greatest sound in the world. And it wasn't really very cool to regard yourself as an entertainer and to do "a show".'

When their audiences began participating in performances by singing along, the band initially felt some resistance, but after one memorable night in Britain's Midlands during their 'Day at the Races' tour in 1977, they decided to embrace the situation. 'We thought, hang on, this is actually something great – this is exceptional. We've got an audience who want to participate in every way – they want to perform with us. So let's encourage them to do just that.' So, with the writing and creation of both the 'We Will Rock You' and 'We Are the Champions' tracks for the *News of the World* album later the same year, the audience *did* in fact become part of the show. And it has been that way ever since. The result was a unique kind of organic energy rocketing Queen shows into a new place.

Unusually at the time, from the beginning a central belief of the band had always been that rock music was an entertainment, that they were entertainers and that their gigs would be about making people feel something; to communicate the emotions – the passion – embodied in their music by putting on a real show. According to May: 'To get it across, we needed every device and it's actually in one of our songs: "Let Me Entertain You" [1978]. It says: "I'LL PULL YOU AND I'LL PILL YOU, I'LL CRUELA DE VIL YOU, AND TO THRILL YOU, I'LL USE ANY DEVICE!" And that's exactly what we thought. We wanted the best sound, the best staging, the best lights, to have the moods put across that corresponded with the songs.'

STUFISH,
Queen + Adam Lambert world tour,
Vancouver,
June 2014

'Now I'm Here': the moment at the beginning of the show where the front kabuki curtain dropped and was sucked up into the centre of the lighting rig creating a dynamic reveal to the show.

STUFISH,
Queen + Adam Lambert
'Rhapsody' world tour,
Seoul, South Korea,
January 2020

'39': Brian May addresses the crowd during his acoustic solo performance. The 16,000-strong audience held up their phones to create a sea of twinkling lights to accompany this intimate moment in the show.

Queen's now iconic stages, however, are the result of an evolution that took years. Roger Taylor explains: 'In the early days, nobody really had a massive stage set. What we call a set now was really all about lights. Visually, it was just lights, and obviously the more lights you had, the better it was. But a lot of people, I think, used lights in the wrong way. They had all these colours going on. It's really quite good to use only one or two colours at once. I think we sort of got that from an early stage. I think we understood lights very well.' Even from the beginning, and unlike many other bands, Queen understood that the multisensory experience their shows had become had to complement, not distract from, the songs. Taylor continues: 'We had lots of lights, but a simple colour palette. If you've got 300 lamps that are all green, it looks pretty good. And we always had a good sense of the power of a single, very powerful spotlight. That magic circle of white, which can be as effective as 1,000 lights, in a different way. It's understanding the dynamics, for the drama of the thing.'

Queen uses the dynamics of varying production qualities very effectively. May elaborates: 'It comes to a point where we think, okay, we've blasted them to death, now we can be intimate; and I go forward, and sit down on a stool at the very edge of the end of the catwalk. And suddenly, the whole dynamic is completely different. Suddenly, I'm alone and vulnerable right in the middle of that crowd of people. And it's a completely different response, a completely different atmosphere.'

Queen understood that the multisensory experience their shows had become had to complement, not distract from, the songs

Keeping it Big, Simple and Wonderful

As the years went on, Queen ploughed their earnings back into the productions, pushing the stage technology as far as they could. They were the first to do the big shows, beginning in the late 1970s, to generate a universe on that one night that would involve the audience and make them feel they were seeing something they had never seen before.

In 1977, for the 'A Day at the Races' tour, they created one of the first mobile lighting rigs, in the shape of a gigantic crown, which rose to reveal the stage. It was subsequently used for their 'News of the World' tour the same year. Taylor remembers: 'We also had other rigs that we nicknamed "the BIC razors", used for "The Game" and "Flash Gordon" tours (1980–81). They looked like disposable razors. They had a bank of lights at the top and hung at a 45-degree angle. Then they had a chain hanging down with a seat and a single spotlight operator in a chair in mid-air. And those things would fly all over the place. We had seven of them and they were incredibly effective. The lights just danced, and people didn't know what they were looking at when they first saw them because they'd never seen the lights move before.'

Early stage technology, including lighting, was analogue, which by necessity incorporated an element of human touch that is now for the most part absent with electronic lights and LEDs. Although the digital technology allows for an immense amount of control and creativity, Queen still try to incorporate the simplicity and physicality of the analogue technology into the staging. May says: 'We keep as much analogue technology in there as we can, consistent with being able to do the wonderful things which digital enables you to do. But you try to reintroduce the magic of what analogue gives you because we are analogue creatures, we're not built digitally, and so that's why it hits a chord with us.' The multisensory effect of incandescent light bulbs, for example, helps their performance. He continues: 'We like to have a few incandescent bulbs around, bulbs that glow and take a while to stop glowing, because they give out a bit of heat. It's all very different from these very clinical electronic lights, LEDs and so forth. So we try to keep them because that heat, and that humanity, is part of where we come from.' The heat generated by one of their early, giant lighting rigs, first used during the 'Jazz Tour' in 1978, was immense, but as he explains, 'The heat generated by that array was at the limit of what you could stand, to be honest, but it generated a heat which helped the show, it gave us a kind of extra physical power. And when the top part of that "pizza oven" was turned on its heel, the audience felt it too; they felt real heat like it was the sun coming on them. And that made a difference to the show.'

Whether they manipulate space and mood in service to their music using simple lights and physical stagecraft or, as now, with the full panoply of digital technology, the music is what drives everything, and everything in the production surrounds the music

in a way that makes it connect emotionally with the audience. Taylor believes this is one of the factors that creates the instantly recognisable look of a Queen show. 'Hopefully it looks beautiful and rich, but effective. It's so important to be effective. You have to do it big, but also be able to highlight the actual players. Sometimes the sets these days can overwhelm the act and you're trying to spot where the artist is. The design should really always have that focus towards the act.' At the same time, from the performers' point of view, 'The design has to look good for the audience, but it also needs to be the thing that empowers the band to make us look big in the room. It gets the celebration rhythmically bound to the music.'

The uniquely synergistic quality of Queen's music and staging is part of their power and popularity. Like all artists, they are influenced by everything they see, including the architecture they put together on the stage. But they are most influenced by the emotions they feel in their relationships, and exploring those and expressing them in ways that hook other people in. May explains: 'The songs give a voice to feelings. That's why our songs connect, because they are very personal. They're about the normal, vulnerable people that we are the same as everybody else is. "I Want to Break Free" [1984]. "I Want It All" [1989]. "Bohemian Rhapsody" [1975] in its way is, of course, a very personal story. So it's the personal, the small stuff, that makes the scene that generates the big stuff. When you're on stage, doing a show, what you're doing is triggering people's feelings which are already inside them. We are so lucky, having been a group that has had those hits, that have connected with people over the years.'

STUFISH,
Queen + Adam Lambert world tour,
Vancouver,
June 2014

'Fat Bottomed Girls': the centre feature of this set was the iconic 'Q' from the Queen crest, surrounded by a rectangular array of moving lights and tungsten 'blinder' lights. The 'Q' itself was a kinetic truss structure that contained moving lighting and framed a central LED screen.

'Hammer to Fall': the set concept was based on an architectural bas-relief oculus. With a radial lighting rig as the backwall surrounding an oval screen, the design created a real 3D sculptural look. The form was generated in Rhino 3D with Grasshopper to explore the false-perspective effect.

Ideally, the stage allows the boundary between performers and audience to be broken down, and the space to be manipulated at the performers' will. STUFISH has done that in different ways throughout the years with Queen since their first collaboration with the band in 2001 with the musical *We Will Rock You,* and continuing with Queen + Paul Rogers (2004–9) and then Queen + Adam Lambert (2012–present), with screens, catwalks, multiple levels, lifts, the B stages, stage extensions and different steps on the drum riser. The increasing flexibility of the physical as well as technological staging allows the show to vary visually. Taylor says: 'I think the beauty of it is that it really looks like a completely different show each time and it has a different visual impact. So having the sets and the different architecture in the sets with ramps, where the singer can compose himself above or below the drums, where Brian can fly into the roof – it's just fantastic.'

May agrees, and elaborates: 'The fact that you can put me on an asteroid and send me up into space, and then I can come down and interact with the people on the left and right, and then go out among them, and actually bring it close up in their faces – that gives me a whole different kind of landscape. You actually have a stage that has more than three dimensions, because you can make it look so many different ways.'

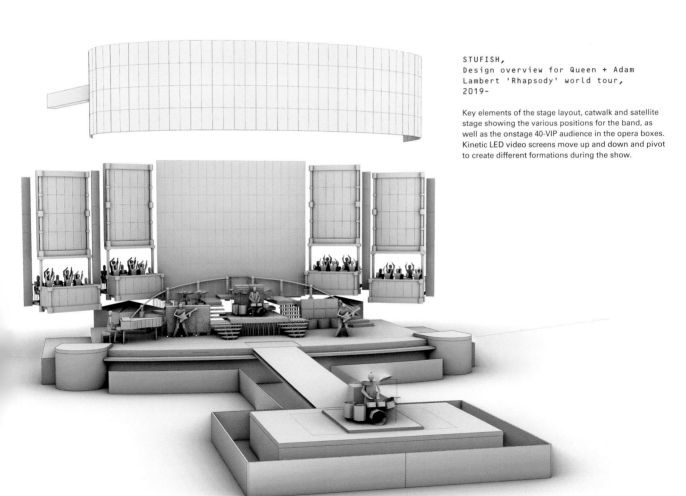

STUFISH,
Design overview for Queen + Adam Lambert 'Rhapsody' world tour, 2019-

Key elements of the stage layout, catwalk and satellite stage showing the various positions for the band, as well as the onstage 40-VIP audience in the opera boxes. Kinetic LED video screens move up and down and pivot to create different formations during the show.

In this sense, what can be done when the digital technology is added is, in May's words, 'monstrously inviting'. He goes on to explain: 'It's a kind of Magic Kingdom. You just can do so much in that space. We play these parts, it's fun to do that. One moment we're big, rock stars strutting around this stage, which we've created and that STUFISH have created with us.' And during the shift from grand spectacle to intimacy, 'I love that when I walk down to the front, the feeling is spine chilling, because the audience sense the incredible change of dynamic that happens. Of course, it's all accentuated with the lighting, colours and shapes and shafts of light.'

The advent of giant LED screens has made an enormous difference in the band's ability to project themselves into larger spaces, where previously it was very hard to emote to the full scale of the space. Since screens have become a canvas for content as well as a way of magnifying the performers, Taylor says that 'you can build things on those screens that add a whole new level to a production, not just a band thrashing away with a load of lights, you can make little worlds with screens. And of course, you can also move the screens, which is fantastic.'

Digital technology has also allowed a blurring between the physical and the virtual. As May says: 'The audience look and they see things that they would swear were solid, like the opera boxes at the back of our recent stage, which actually had real and virtual people in them. What STUFISH have done for us has been monumental and I think pushes the boundaries of staging way far into the future.'

STUFISH,
Queen + Adam Lambert 'Rhapsody' world tour,
Tacoma, Washington,
July 2019

'Love of My Life': the most poignant moment in the show.
As Brian May sings the last few lines of the song, a mirage
of Freddie Mercury emerges out of the smoke to finish the last
few chords, generating a combination of applause and tears.

These arenas become almost tribal or religious experiences, for people to come and worship in the rock music'

Because the Music is King

At the same time the band are well aware that they can perform effectively on a small, two-dimensional stage without depth. May remembers: 'We had nothing when we did Live Aid [13 July 1985]. We had none of our own staging there. We had none of our own lights or sound-effects gear. And we were able to do it. I think you can do music powerful enough to work in any situation. If it's the right song and the right singer, and you feel passion, that's what it's about. But if you want to maximise the effect and the joy, the experience of going to a concert, then you do stage it, and you go to town as far as you can.' But however simple a stage set seems to be, he explains, you can never have no production; you are always making a decision: 'Whenever you step on that stage, whenever you turn on an amp, whenever you switch on a light, you're making decisions about how you want to come across. And sometimes, if you get it right, it's real magic.'

Neither May nor Taylor thinks there is a substitute for that magic, which only happens during a live experience. Taylor feels virtual performances are 'a stop-gap measure, and I don't think the hunger for real live shows will stop. Joyous, celebratory rock-and-roll shows and festivals will be so great when all this pestilence has gone. I think it's going to come back with such a bang.'

May muses: 'Our touring shows are essentially building a form for the music. In the olden days, you would build a church for a religious collection. I really like the concept that these shows are like a portable church going around the world. Like a shrine. These arenas become almost tribal or religious experiences, for people to come and worship in the rock music.' ₪

This article is based on a tele-video interview with Brian May and Roger Taylor on 14 January 2021.

STUFISH,
Queen + Adam Lambert
'News of the World' tour,
Las Vegas, Nevada,
June 2017

'We Will Rock You': a large oval lighting rig called 'The Halo' was lifted up by 'Frank the Robot' to reveal the band. Containing 100 moving lights, it emulated Queen's historic lighting rigs, but with a new twist. The lights all pulsed in red to the anthemic beat of the song.

FROM ANOTHER PERSPECTIVE

A Word from
⚠ Editor Neil Spiller

HAMMERSMITH APOLLO

A SAVAGE SPLENDOUR

**Foster Wilson Architects,
Hammersmith Apollo refurbishment,
London, 2013**

The ground-floor foyer and upper circle bar areas are
punctuated by a spectacular sensuous void that visually
connects them, affording views between them.

This ◫ is about the performative nature of architecture and the design of processes and machinery that encourage interaction between audience and act. This choreography of staging, its construction, movement and transience is tailored to the venues that will host it. There is a fleeting symbiosis between the site and set and it is this combination of the venue and the show that becomes fixed in the crowd's mind and memory, often for life. This is particularly true for the fans of rock bands.

I experienced my first 'Megaton surprise' on 12 March 1976 at what was then known as the Empire Pool, Wembley. A relatively daring building created by the notable English engineer Sir Owen Williams (1890–1969), completed in 1934. Its structure mainly comprises large cantilevers that meet at its centre so as not to require intermediate columns punctuating its span. It was originally designed as a huge swimming pool but has not been used for this purpose since the 1948 Olympic Games. When used for music concerts its capacity is 12,500 people and on this occasion it was packed.

Come Taste the Band

It was my first gig, and the band was Deep Purple – proud owners of the moniker 'loudest band in the world', at 117 decibels in 1972, according to the *Guinness Book of Records* at the time. They were one of the triumvirate of great and innovative rock bands that roamed the world, behemoth-like, along with Black Sabbath and Led Zeppelin. They were sufficiently popular for the sixth-formers in my provincial Canterbury school (75 miles (120 kilometres) from Wembley) to hire a coach and driver for the evening to get us there and back. So, after a few cans of cider on the journey, there I was at Wembley suitably attired in platform shoes and green trousers that my mother called 'Oxford bags' (a loose-fitting baggy form of trousers favoured by members of the University of Oxford from the mid-1920s to around the 1950s), woollen tank top and cheesecloth shirt with a huge floppy collar and a huge floppy hippie haircut, looking like every other male teenager of the time. Not being a live football punter unless it's on telly, I had never experienced such a large, excited crowd, and the sight of the heavy-metal diaspora congregating was mind-boggling.

This was a much simpler time – no band websites, no YouTube, no rock webzines; albums had to be bought in a record shop, and news of bands was gleaned through music newspapers like *Sounds* or the *New Musical Express*. No big screens, no mobile-phone videos, no VIP packages. Much was made of dry ice, bars were ridiculously packed and toilets dirty with lengthy queues (particularly when the support band was on), the band itself mere specks on the horizon, but good to be in the same – albeit massive – room as one's heroes. But the sound, oh my word, the SOUND. As the first song hit me, my

Hammersmith Odeon front façade,
London,
4 June 1980

Before the doors to a gig were opened, the denim/leather-clad and hairy congregation would shuffle about and queue, often drunkenly but good-naturedly waiting for admission to the Temple.

ears panicked and I could not make out which song was being played. My ears rang for three days after, but I'd been bitten by the bug. Unbeknown to me at the time, the fourth incarnation of Deep Purple that played that night was only a few nights off self-destruction, marred by some members' drug habits. Yet the occasion, the ritual, the architecture, the performance, the audience and the thrill of it all continue in my memory so many decades later. This is what entertainment architecture is all about: making memories.

For a couple of years I made a few local forays to see bands: Samson with the then unknown singer Bruce Dickinson (subsequently Iron Maiden) at the University of Kent, and a trip to the Leas Cliff Hall in Folkestone to see the fledgling Whitesnake, formed by ex-Deep Purple vocalist David Coverdale, who had fronted the band that night at Wembley. They had just released the album *North Winds*. On the track 'Breakdown' Coverdale reminisces about that 1976 Deep Purple world tour in not very flattering terms.

The Great Temple at the Centre of the Gyratory System

Whilst the Empire Pool, with its subsequent renamings, has had many high points that have entered music mythology, there is a relatively intimate venue that trumps it in the UK's history

This was a much simpler time – no band websites, no YouTube, no rock webzines

The history of Hammersmith Odeon reads like a who's who of musical entertainment. Imagine any famous rock band from the 1960s onwards and the chances are they have played here, probably numerous times over the years

Hammersmith Odeon set up for a Rush concert in May 1979

The view from above the drum kit shows the relationship between audience and stage.

Foster Wilson Architects, Hammersmith Apollo refurbishment, London, 2013

The upstairs long curving circle bar is daylit by Art Deco etched window panels created for Robert Crombie's original design of the building (completed 1932).

of rock and roll: London's Hammersmith Odeon. Designed by Robert Crombie in the flamboyant Art Deco style, this building was originally completed in 1932. First called the Gaumont Palace, it has had many other names since, including its current manifestation as the Eventim Apollo; but to rock fans of my generation, it will always be the 'Odeon'.

My next trip to London to commune with the hairy hordes was in 1978, to see one of the Canadian band Rush's first gigs in the UK. This was the first time I experienced the dilapidated interiors of the 'Odeon', much marred by cigarette butt burns, spilt beer, cheap carpets and indiscriminate overpainting, only hints of its illustrious architectural past punctuating its spaces. Even so, to me and the thousands of loud-music lovers it was a tawdry temple of worship.

The history of Hammersmith Odeon reads like a who's who of musical entertainment. Imagine any famous rock band from the 1960s onwards and the chances are they have played here, probably numerous times over the years. It was, for example, the place where David Bowie announced the end of his Ziggy Stardust persona on 3 July 1973. Many live albums have been recorded here too. Two of the most well known, in the hard-rock genre, are Motorhead's *No Sleep 'til Hammersmith* (1981) and Whitesnake's *Live...in the Heart of the City*

(1980). A quick Google search will confirm the numerous iconic events that have occurred here. Other moments synonymous with the building, in my mind, include my best friend at the time falling asleep next to me (we'd had a few!), halfway through a cheroot, and setting fire to his Afghan coat, which he was wearing during a Black Sabbath concert. Security extracted him expertly from the crowd, venue and coat and let him back in, the coat of course ruined by flames and water. It was winter and the journey back to southeast Kent on the Milk Train was fraught with four-letter-worded exclamations of coldness and suspected frostbite; only the smothering of himself with the as yet unsold morning papers, also on the train, placated his distress. More significant personal events/concerts at the Odeon include bands such as Whitesnake on numerous occasions, Ozzy Osbourne, Ritchie Blackmore's Rainbow, Budgie, Blue Öyster Cult, Angel Witch, Magnum and many others. Many of my memories of these events are reinforced by memories of the Odeon itself, the touch of its seating, the waits at the bar, the fire curtain, the roar of the crowd and, subsequently, the terrible emerging hangover, the crowded last tube and long walk home with ringing ears in the early hours. I loved it! The building is engrained in my psyche.

**Foster Wilson Architects,
Hammersmith Apollo refurbishment,
London, 2013**

above: The spruced-up exterior of the venue and its colourfully lit façade contrasts well with its formerly gritty appearance in the 1970s and 1980s.

right: The curve and rake of the new seating affords a good viewing angle to all the audience.

Now the interiors are resplendent with their beautiful 1930s glamour that does justice to the building's Grade II* listing rating – the second most important building conservation category in the UK

The Art of Decorating the Deco
Foster Wilson Architects have been working with the building owners, AEG Live and CTS Eventim to restore this legendary Grade II* listed live entertainment venue, through a project of many phases.

Commencing in 2012, the first, main objective was to rejuvenate the front-of-house areas and the auditorium. Edmund Wilson – who led the restoration project together with his fellow partner in the practice, Jonathan Size – remarks: 'The building is fascinating – as a very considered piece of Art Deco architecture and an auditorium that really works for live bands, with such a wide stage.'[1] A series of renovations were made including, amongst others, remaking some of the fixtures and fittings to the original designs, matching the original colour schemes of each space, restoring Art Deco plasterwork, revealing existing windows in the circle and giving the front façade a new lighting scheme.

Commencing in 2012, the first, main objective was to rejuvenate the front-of-house areas and the auditorium

'Part of the reason everything is so well preserved,' comments Wilson, 'is that the whole venue was covered in brown paint in the 1960s but nothing was removed – we mostly rolled back the sticky carpets, went back to the original colour scheme (full of green, purple, silver and gold) and changed the 1980s bars.'[2] During this process exciting discoveries were made, a particularly enjoyable one being the revealing of original Deco-patterned terrazzo flooring in the foyer/bar area. Further happy surprises were sculptor Newbury Abbot Trent's friezes, two staircases (one on either side of the stage) made of marble, plus glazing in the Art Deco style – all patiently waiting to be woken up and rejuvenated. Now the interiors are resplendent with their beautiful 1930s glamour that does justice to the building's Grade II* listing rating – the second most important building conservation category in the UK. Now the venue shines like a diamond in the frenetic rough of Hammersmith – a beacon of millions of memories.

Today the more popular acts play the O2, the former Millennium Dome in Southeast London – a large Dutch cap of a building created by the Richard Rogers Partnership to house the UK's celebrations for the turn of the new century. The last time I went to a rock concert it was there. The crowd, polite, queued nicely for their airport-like security check; our VIP tickets funnelled us off towards our private box; our own personal waiter/barman introduced himself and started pouring drinks; there was plenty of room around us, no queues in the lavatories, good views, great sound that did not damage the ears. A thoroughly enjoyable experience close to where I live. However, my heart will always belong at the Hammersmith Odeon.

Halcyon days! ◮

Notes
1. Email correspondence between Neil Spiller and Edmund Wilson, 18 November 2020.
2. *Ibid.*

S. Leonard Auerbach is the founder and Director of Design of Auerbach Pollock Friedlander, and brings over 50 years of professional experience and international expertise in theatre consulting to his practice. His approach to theatre, architectural lighting, audio-video and multimedia consulting combines a background in architecture with his scenic and theatrical lighting design experience gained in New York and at leading regional theatres. With hundreds of projects to his credit, his leadership and personal involvement assures the highest level of design and quality of work. He is an alumni and founder of the Carnegie Mellon University Theatre Architecture Studio.

Victoria Broackes is Director of the London Design Biennale and Senior Curator for the Victoria and Albert Museum Department of Theatre and Performance. She was V&A Curator of the 'Pink Floyd: Their Mortal Remains' exhibition (2017) and co-curator of 'You Say You Want a Revolution? 1966–70' and 'David Bowie Is', the fastest selling exhibition in the V&A's history which attracted over two million visitors around the world. She is a trustee of the Handel & Hendrix museum in London, an alumni member of the Court of the Royal College of Art (RCA) and of the Court of the Goldsmiths' Company.

Sir Peter Cook was a founder of Archigram in the 1960s, taught at the Architectural Association (AA) in London from 1964 to 1990, and was a professor at the Stadelschule, Frankfurt, from 1984 to 2009. He was Professor and Chair of the Bartlett School of Architecture, University College London (UCL) from 1990 to 2006, and is a RIBA Royal Gold Medalist (with Archigram). He has authored nine books, and his drawings are in the collections of the Museum of Modern Art (MoMA) in New York, Deutsches Architekturmuseum (DAM) in Frankfurt, Centre Pompidou in Paris and the FRAC Centre in Orléans, France. His built works include the Kunsthaus Graz (2003) with Colin Fournier, and with his current practice CRAB studio the departments of Law and Central Administration at the University of Vienna

(2013), Abedian School of Architecture at Bond University, Gold Coast, Australia (2014) and the Drawing Studio at the Arts University Bournemouth (2016). He was knighted for services to architecture in 2007.

Adam Davis is Chief Creative Officer at TAIT. With an innate passion for creating, he has cemented his success within the live entertainment industry by developing revolutionary technologies and unique design concepts for world-class experiences. At TAIT he manages a team of skilled live event specialists including engineers, designers, scenic artists, software developers, fabricators and more. Since joining the company in 1997, he has propelled the company from what was once a team of less than a dozen individuals into a mounting fleet of TAIT experts worldwide. Under his leadership, TAIT has taken part in productions in over 30 countries, all seven continents and even outer space.

Haidy Geismar is Professor of Anthropology at UCL. She is also the curator of the UCL Ethnography Collections, co-directs the Digital Anthropology Programme, and is Faculty Vice Dean (Strategic Projects) developing a new School for Cultural and Creative Industries as part of UCL's new campus in the Olympic Park in East London. Her research focuses on museums and collections as sites of knowledge and value production, and she has written on a wide range of topics including the art market, post-colonial museologies, the production of indigenous intellectual and cultural property, the history of ethnographic collections, and the impact of digitisation in museums. Her most recent book is *Museum Object Lessons for the Digital Age* (UCL Press, 2018).

Robert Kronenburg is an architect and Emeritus Roscoe Chair of Architecture at the University of Liverpool. His research explores innovative forms of architectural design and popular music. He is a past Fulbright fellow and has co-curated exhibitions for the Vitra Design Museum in Weil-Am-Rhein, Germany, as well as at the Royal Institute of British Architects (RIBA) and Building Centre in London. His books have been translated into French, German, Spanish, Japanese and Chinese, and include *Flexible: Architecture that Responds to Change* (Laurence King, 2007) and *Architecture in Motion: The History and Development of Portable Building* (Routledge, 2014). His most recent book is *This Must Be The Place: An Architectural History of Popular Music Performance Venues* (Bloomsbury, 2019).

Ric Lipson is a Partner at STUFISH Entertainment Architects and an ARB-registered architect. He is a show-maker who has design and production experience across the live entertainment industry. He has worked with many global artists over the years, from Madonna to Beyoncé and U2.

Ash Nehru had a good thing going in the games industry, but messed it up by quitting to make virtual go-go-dancing robots for raves, write DJ software and travel the world performing. Failing miserably at this, in 2003 he co-founded United Visual Artists, creating live shows and installations, and writing software that was eventually spun off into a moderately successful company called Disguise. He now splits his time between blue-sky research and posting pictures of his dinner on Instagram.

Aubrey Powell co-founded the album cover design company Hipgnosis with Storm Thorgerson in 1967. Hipgnosis created some of the most innovative and surreal record cover art of the 1960s, 1970s and 1980s for many of the big-name rock bands of the era including Pink Floyd, Led Zeppelin, Paul McCartney, Genesis, 10cc, Peter Gabriel, Styx, Syd Barrett and Black Sabbath. The company was nominated for Grammy Awards five times. Powell was the creative director of the bestselling exhibition 'Pink Floyd: Their Mortal Remains' at the V&A in London. He also directs documentaries, live multi-camera shoots and feature films.

Neil Thomas is the founder and Director of innovative engineering practice Atelier One. He believes in a holistic approach to

structural design, with active engagement throughout the design process. Form must follow function – there cannot be a disconnect between architecture and engineering. He has pioneered the use of a number of innovative materials, most recently advocating the use of carbon fibre to reduce the weight of touring structures. It is this approach that resulted in his being awarded the International Association for Bridge and Structural Engineering (IABSE) Milne Medal in 2019.

Willie Williams creates visual environments for live events and concert tours. He is best known for his longstanding creative relationship with the rock band U2. Merging lighting, video imagery and scenic elements into a single visual discipline, his work has been highly regarded as conceptually and technologically groundbreaking.

Patrick Woodroffe is a senior partner of the international lighting design consultancy Woodroffe Bassett Design (WBD). Over the last 40 years he has created the lighting for rock concerts, operas, ballet, film, architecture and special events. He has been the lighting designer and creative director for the Rolling Stones since 1982, he lit the London Olympic and Paralympic Games opening and closing ceremonies, and in 2014 was awarded an OBE for a lifetime of services to the arts.

MAciej Woroniecki is a partner at STUFISH. His work focuses on the intersection of performance and experience. At STUFISH, over the past decade he has implemented innovative design solutions to drive entertainment architecture towards new and immersive typologies. He has an extended catalogue of work experience around the world at a wide variety of scales. A graduate of the AA School of Architecture, he has lectured and taught at the University of Liechtenstein and University of Westminster as well as at the AA.

What is *Architectural Design*?

Founded in 1930, *Architectural Design* (△) is an influential and prestigious publication. It combines the currency and topicality of a newsstand journal with the rigour and production qualities of a book. With an almost unrivalled reputation worldwide, it is consistently at the forefront of cultural thought and design.

Issues of △ are edited either by the journal Editor, Neil Spiller, or by an invited Guest-Editor. Renowned for being at the leading edge of design and new technologies, △ also covers themes as diverse as architectural history, the environment, interior design, landscape architecture and urban design.

Provocative and pioneering, △ inspires theoretical, creative and technological advances. It questions the outcome of technical innovations as well as the far-reaching social, cultural and environmental challenges that present themselves today.

For further information on △, subscriptions and purchasing single issues see:

https://onlinelibrary.wiley.com/journal/15542769

Volume 90 No 6
ISBN 978 1119 685371

Volume 91 No 1
ISBN 978 1119 717669

Volume 91 No 2
ISBN 978 1119 717485

Volume 91 No 3
ISBN 978 1119 747222

Volume 91 No 4
ISBN 978 1119 717522

Volume 91 No 5
ISBN 978 1119 717706